Drawing Them In or Driving Them Away?

Developing a Christlike Character That Commits to Love, Cares for the Fallen, Cultivates Peace, and Compels the Lost to Christ

LAMBERT W. GATES, SR.

Dedication

To those who carry unseen wounds,
yet still choose to love.

To every believer whose life whispers Christ
more loudly than their lips.

And to the ones we've driven away—
may our hearts be healed,
our witness made whole,
and our lives once again
draw them in.

Drawing Them In or Driving Them Away?: Developing a Christlike Character That Commits to Love, Cares for the Fallen, Cultivates Peace, and Compels the Lost to Christ

Copyright © 2025 by Lambert W. Gates, Sr.

All rights reserved. No part of this book may be reproduced, stored in a retrieval system, or transmitted in any form or by any means, electronic, mechanical, photocopying, recording, or otherwise, without prior written permission from the publisher.

For permissions or bulk orders, please contact:

L.W. Gates Ministries

4900 E. 38th Street

Indianapolis, IN 46218

ISBN: 979-8-9929969-3-7

Scripture quotations marked AMP are taken from the Amplified® Bible (AMP), Copyright © 2015 by The Lockman Foundation. Used by permission. lockman.org.

Scripture quotations marked AMPC are taken from the Amplified® Bible (AMPC), Copyright © 1954, 1958, 1962, 1964, 1965, 1987 by The Lockman Foundation. Used by permission. lockman.org.

Scripture quotations marked CEB are taken from the COMMON ENGLISH BIBLE. © Copyright 2011 COMMON ENGLISH BIBLE. All rights reserved. Used by permission. (www.CommonEnglishBible.com).

Scripture quotations marked KJV are taken from The Authorized (King James) Version. Rights in the Authorized Version in the United Kingdom are vested in the Crown. Reproduced by permission of the Crown's patentee, Cambridge University Press.

Scripture quotations marked NIV are taken from the Holy Bible, New International Version®, NIV®. Copyright © 1973, 1978, 1984, 2011 by Biblica, Inc.™ Used by permission of Zondervan. All rights reserved worldwide. www.zondervan.com. The "NIV" and "New International Version" are trademarks registered in the United States Patent and Trademark Office by Biblica, Inc.™

Scripture quotations marked NKJV are taken from the New King James Version®. Copyright © 1982 by Thomas Nelson. Used by permission. All rights reserved.

Table of Contents

Introduction 11

1. The Saints Are Not Kind 15
   We Like a Good Lynching in the Church....................16
   Selfishness: The Reason Why We Like
   a Good Lynching 18
   Stop Exposing and Start Loving Others........................18
   When People Call for Others to Be Punished
   but Forget They Got Helped 20
   We Act Holy and Then We Judge Others 21
   Gossiping...24
   The Prevalence of Pride in Keeping
   People Offended & Odds...25

2. The Disposition of the Believer 29
   What is a Disposition? 30
   Our Thinking Determines Our Disposition 32
   You Have the Holy Ghost…
   but Where's the Transformation? 33
   Do Bad Things Keep Happening to You?
   Check Your Disposition! 37
   God's Standard Never Gives You the
   Green Light to Go Off!..44
   Do You Really Believe God Can Change
   Your Contentious Character? 46

3. What Spiritual Maturity Looks Like in the Believer's Disposition 49

What Does the Disposition of a
Mature Believer Look Like? 51

  Strengthening the Brethren 52

  Being Led by God's Word, Not Emotions 52

  Preferring Others Over Ourselves 53

  Seeing & Trying to Understand Others 55

  Restoring Rather Than Exposing Saints
  Who Stumble 56

  Doing Good to Those Who Wrong You 59

Want True Transformation?
Don't Get Distracted by Externals 62

4. Empathy: The Key Ingredient of the Mature Believer's Disposition 65

5. Still a Babe After Years of Salvation? Something's Wrong! 73

What Does the Disposition of a Babe
in Christ Look Like? 74

  Out-of-control Emotions 75

  Lack of Concern for Brothers and Sisters 76

  Inconsistency in the Things of God 77

  Inability to Receive Correction 78

  Easily Conforming to Worldly Influences 79

  Competing with Others 81

Are Carnality, Comfort & Convenience Keeping You Stuck in the Babe Stage? 82

Suffering & Sacrifice: A Part of the Mature-in-Christ Package 84

Moving on to Maturity is a Choice You Must Make! ... 85

The Charge to Mature and Grow Up! 88

6. The Malpractice of Ministry Leaders Lacking Maturity 91

7. Going on to Perfection: Making the Commitment to Grow Into a Mature Believer 97

How to Move on to Perfection 99

    Prayer 99

    Self-reflection 100

    Refusing to Conform to the World 100

    Acknowledgement of Our Sinfulness 101

    Extending the Grace You've Received to Others 102

    A Call to Commit to the Transformation 102

Acknowledgments

This book was birthed in prayer, reflection, and the often-painful awareness of how easily the Church can bless or bruise, heal or harm, draw in or drive away.

I give honor to the countless saints—both known and unknown—whose quiet witness shaped my own. Your lives were sermons I never forgot.

To my beloved wife, children, and grandchildren—thank you for anchoring me in love and reminding me daily what it means to live with compassion and grace. You are my first congregation, my lifelong joy.

To my trusted assistants, armor bearers, and ministry team—you carry burdens few ever see. Your faithfulness behind the scenes has allowed me to serve publicly with strength and peace.

To Dr. Shannon Comier, thank you for your editorial clarity and visionary care. And to the design team and publishing partners who brought this project to life— your excellence shines through every page.

Finally, to those who have ever felt pushed away by imperfect people representing a perfect Christ—this work is for you. May our failures be transformed into invitations, and may love lead us all home.

Introduction

I have a serious question for you. Why aren't people more attracted to you? Now, when I ask this question, I don't mean 'attracted' in the sense of romantic attraction. Instead, I am referring to spiritual attraction. Why aren't more people coming to Christ through you? Why aren't there people coming to you in church and asking you to disciple or spiritually mentor them? I could also ask this question with regard to your ability to get along with those you worship with in your community of faith. Why don't more people come to you to invite you to participate on teams or committees? Why are you the last person people want to approach with an opportunity to contribute to a project, event, or ministry task? Why aren't you making the impact with others in ministry that you would like to be able to make? Why don't people want you around?

Drawing Them In or Driving Them Away?

What is it about you that's just not that attractive to other people? Let me gently suggest that your lack of attractiveness might have something to do with your disposition. I want you to strongly consider whether you have a disposition that looks like the character of Christ or whether you have a disposition all your own that reflects your personal opinions, thoughts, and attitudes. Only one of these dispositions is attractive to others, and it's not the one that looks more like you. It is the one that looks more like Christ.

This question of disposition brings us to a deeper reflection. Brothers and sisters, we are supposed to not just be Christians but act like it. We are called to be Christ-like, not just in our minds but in ways that others can see – in visible expressions where people experience Christ's love, mercy, care, understanding, and restoration through our lives. When you think about it, in order for Christ to be a suitable sacrifice, He took on the frailty of our flesh (John 1:14). He was tempted in all points as we are, yet without sin (Hebrews 4:15). Jesus passed the test that Adam flunked. He identified with us to the point that He was willing to be broken for us. If we are to be Christ-like, should we not treat our brothers and sisters the same way? How far are we willing to go to ensure that others are forgiven, healed, and restored to wholeness? Are we willing to give up the disposition driven by our personal attitude and carnal desires in order to take on the character and disposition of Christ? I'm not suggesting that doing so is easy, but I am suggesting that this should be the goal of those who call themselves followers of Christ. This pursuit is what defines the disposition of a mature believer.

I wrote this book not only as a challenge to laity but to leaders, too. Leaders are not immune to lacking the disposition of mature believers. We can be in all types of ministry positions and have all manner of titles and responsibilities and still not reflect Christ's disposition. This is why each of us must constantly engage in self-reflection, measuring ourselves against the character of Christ – even me. I never mean to sound self-righteous; I'm not immune to anything any other leader experiences. In fact, I struggle with much of what I write to other leaders and members about, so as I preach to others, I am preaching to myself. Many times, I tell my members that I'm the mailman who delivers all the mail to them, but just know when I get home, there's a mailbox with bills in it for me, too.

The aim of this book is to challenge believers of all stages of Christianity, titles, ranks, and responsibilities who are supposed to be born again and formed in Christ—who are supposed to be walking according to the image of Christ—to stop merely talking this way and actually begin living it. It is to lead people like you in asking important self-reflective questions like, "When will I finally start actualizing the mentality and ways of Christ so that I am more Christ-like?" "When will I yield to God's Word and allow my attitudes and actions to be guided purely by love?" Everything that Christ did was motivated by love, and since we are to reflect Him in our character and disposition, so should we who call ourselves "Christians."

If we avoid this spiritual maturity and continue operating in self-interest, we will never become the city that is set upon a hill—set apart and shining brightly—that Christ invited us to be. We won't differentiate ourselves from the world in terms of our capacity to love. This lack of differentiation will ultimately affect the church's mission by thwarting our witness and ability to win souls. It will also cause the church of Jesus Christ to not be a safe place. One of my spiritual fathers preached a message about how each local church is a branch office of heaven. People ought to be able to go into church and find a haven, a safe space from this world. However, how can they enter into the church and find safety and peace when they come in and see us bickering, fighting, condemning one another, and throwing each other away? We have looked at the church in our tradition more often as a place of exceptionalism. But we must also see it as a refuge—a place of healing and welcome. It has been our sanctuary and escape from the world. However, we must create an inviting, accepting, understanding, and nonjudgmental atmosphere in the church in order to be attractive to those who are seeking to connect with Christ in His house.

As you work your way through the principles I present in this book, I encourage you to reflect on how you can do more to manifest the disposition of the believer as Christ intended. If you commit to doing so, I can almost guarantee that you will have more ministry impact, more godly influence, be more effective in reaching the unsaved for Christ, become a more trusted listening ear for your struggling brothers and sisters, be more spiritually respected in the things of God, and be more effective in all you do in the kingdom.

May the Lord bless all who embrace the calling to increase in Christ-like disposition, choosing to decrease themselves that He might increase in them.

1
The Saints Are Not Kind
(A Poorly Kept Secret in the Body of Christ!)

I've observed a painful reality over the past several decades of leading in the Lord's church. It's probably something that you've seen, too. In fact, most people see it, but few are willing to talk about it. What is this phenomenon that I've observed? The saints are often not kind.

Instead of operating with kindness, they are often mean, harsh with one another, judgmental, easy to dismiss each other or throw people away, selfish, emotionally driven, and prone to clashing with their brothers and sisters in Christ. None of this reflects who we are called to be after we have been graciously saved by the blood of Jesus, lavished with His goodness and mercy, forgiven for our sin, and given the gift of eternal life. You would expect people who had received such an incredible gift (one that none of us deserves) to walk around so grateful, so full of love, that anyone looking from the outside in would be deeply moved by how we show others the same love, kindness, grace, mercy, care, and forgiveness that Christ showed to us. However, the unfortunate truth is that when people look at the church—and especially when they join and get involved—they often see everything but this.

This lack of kindness, love, and care among believers has become a major area of concern in my pastoral ministry. I am compelled to ask: When does the believer mature to the point that they actually act like a believer and take on the nature of Christ? When will people start doing what the Bible says in Philippians 2:5: "Let this mind be in you which was also in Christ Jesus" (NKJV)? When will we stop operating out of our pre-salvation, natural, carnal mind and start functioning with the mind of Christ?

We Like a Good Lynching in the Church

I've had a bird's-eye view for years, and I'm going to call it like I see it: we tend to like a good lynching in the church. We like to discover the moral wrongdoings of people in the church and watch as they become subject to public judgment. However, in the trial, we don't hope and pray for their restoration to wholeness so they can go and sin no more. Instead, we want to see them punished to the fullest extent! We want to see them lose their title, position, authority, influence, friends, spouse… everything!

I've always wondered why people want their brothers and sisters in Christ to pay for their penalties, but when it comes to their own, they want grace and mercy and expect to be dealt with privately. People don't realize it, but this is the difference between the disposition of a mature believer and a babe. We've got to grow up and understand that everyone in the church has their own sanctification issues that they are struggling with, no matter how holy, pristine, or put-together they appear to be on the surface. Therefore, everyone is going to need understanding, grace, and spiritual support from the church community at some point. There's no need to throw people away. Christ is a forgiver and a restorer, and we should be, too!

When you like to see people get called out for their immoral or sinful attitudes or actions, especially in front of the saints, you have to really examine your heart. Ask yourself, "Why is it that I actually enjoy watching others get exposed?" Then, be self-reflective and honest enough with yourself to give a sincere answer. If you ask me, I believe that people like a good lynching because it makes life a lot easier for us when we can focus on the frailties of others, taking the attention off our own flaws and shortcomings. Rather than using our time feeling convicted and engaging in the arduous process of dying to ourselves and being more Christlike, we distract ourselves by using the downfall of others as entertainment. We know that we are going through our own set of struggles that could have landed us in the same situation—but at least we didn't get caught!

Selfishness: The Reason Why We Like a Good Lynching

At the core of the way that we treat people in the church—rejoicing, whether openly or secretly, in their downfall and moral struggles—is selfishness. We are so selfish in the church! We cling so tightly to our image of holiness and piety that we welcome the chance to appear more righteous by comparison. Just selfish. Pulling away from selfishness should be a daily fight for every believer, and it can only be done by heeding the words of the apostle Paul: "Let this mind be in you which was also in Christ Jesus" (Philippians 2:5, NKJV).

We will never have the disposition of the believer if we don't have the mind of Christ, who emptied Himself for our sake. Paul writes, "but [He] made Himself of no reputation, taking the form of a bondservant, and coming in the likeness of men. And being found in appearance as a man, He humbled Himself and became obedient to the point of death, even the death of the cross" (Philippians 2:7–8, NKJV). Are you emptying yourself for the sake of others? Are you willing to put away selfishness so that others can be saved, healed, and restored? This is the only way we can be Christ-like and manifest God's intended disposition of a believer.

Stop Exposing and Start Loving Others

Everybody wants things to be exposed until they're the ones in the hot seat, trying to keep their own failures under wraps. Once they get into some trouble or their flaws and moral failures get revealed, now all of a sudden, they believe in covering. Consider what covering is and what it means. If I, your pastor or bishop, am your covering, is it only to keep demons off your back, or is it also to keep the destroyers or the vultures away when you are in a vulnerable place? I suggest it's both.

The challenge is that this seems to be a hard concept for people in the church to grasp. Nobody is in favor of showing mercy until they need it themselves. However, the Scripture says in Matthew 5:7, "Blessed are the merciful, for they shall obtain mercy" (NKJV). How do we forget these words of Christ? Now, when I say that we should be merciful, I'm not condoning wickedness. Instead, I'm encouraging you to do what Jesus did about wickedness. He didn't condemn; He forgave and mercifully restored. The very act of restoration acknowledges that something is broken; however, just because something is broken doesn't mean it's garbage or refuse that needs to be thrown out. We have to start pushing back on dealing with others out of condemnation rather than mercy. Showing mercy doesn't make us less holy—it makes us more like Christ.

The highest metric for how holy you are is not how many people you throw away because of their moral failures but how much you love. The Bible says in 1 Peter 4:8, "And above all things have fervent love for one another, for 'love will cover a multitude of sins'" (NKJV). Notice the scripture says that love covers a multitude of faults or sins; it doesn't condone them. It's important to make the distinction between the two.

One of my dear friends said something to me 40 years ago, and I never forgot it: Love is what love does. Again, I take you back to the story of the Good Samaritan. While others overlooked the man who was in need, it was the Samaritan who cared for the man and tended to his needs. The whole principle of the parable was the question Jesus asked: Who was neighbor to him? The one who came to where he was and had compassion on him, demonstrating his love through his actions. I challenge you to do the same. Be neighborly to your brothers and sisters.

When People Call for Others to Be Punished but Forget They Got Helped

So often, I get members who come to me wanting people to be castigated and publicly punished for what they've done in the church. The problem is, they forget the things they themselves have done that were worthy of the same penalty. How easily people forget!

This reminds me of a situation I had in my church. There was a female who had become a little too frisky and disorderly toward a married man in the church. One of the man's family members, a sibling, came into my office, and we had an interaction that I'll never forget. They came and sat down in front of me and said confrontationally, "Are you just going to allow this woman to continue in ministry after she acted this way with my sibling? How could you!" Before I realized what I was saying, I looked at them and said, "The same way I helped you when you got yourself in the struggle you just had not too long ago." Their face dropped, and they were shocked! How easily they had forgotten that only a few weeks before, they had been in my office talking to me about their own moral failures. I did what good pastors do: I prayed with them and helped them get through their dilemma without revealing them or their mistakes to others.

I had personally worked with them, but in their haste to accuse someone else for struggling with the same kind of behavior, they had forgotten their own flaws.

We Act Holy and Then We Judge Others

In the holiness church, we also like to say that we are honest and genuine about who we are. However, the truth is, all of this is part of the fallacy of this wonderful realm of holiness. We are often dishonest with ourselves about who we truly are and dishonest with others. Everybody is walking around with a mask on, presenting a façade of their real selves. We lead with our ideal selves—our polished representatives who appear holy on the outside—the way we want others to view us. We don't share our struggles, our sufferings, our challenging situations, or our sanctification spots, because in our eyes, this might make us appear "less than" to others. We act like we've got it all together, knowing full well that we don't; all kinds of issues are happening behind the scenes of our holiness. And then, we have the unmitigated nerve to judge other people when a piece of their façade falls off and we see one of their flaws, knowing that our own lives are full of them! Help us, Lord, to be more genuine. Help us build a church community where the disposition of the believer reflects Christ, so people do not feel abandoned, isolated, or alone in their struggles.

We must always examine ourselves and engage in self-reflection to ensure that our hearts, minds, and ways are aligned with God and His Word. The apostle Paul speaks of a moment that God designed for us to do just this: communion. In 1 Corinthians 11:18–22, he first addresses a divided church by giving them instructions about the Lord's Supper:

> *18 For first of all, when you come together as a church, I hear that there are divisions among you, and in part I believe it. 19 For there must also be factions among you, that those who are approved may be recognized among you. 20 Therefore when you come together in one place, it is not to eat the Lord's Supper. 21 For in eating, each one takes his own supper ahead of others; and one is hungry and another is drunk. 22 What! Do you not have houses to eat and drink in? Or do you despise the church of God and shame those who have nothing? What shall I say to you? Shall I praise you in this? I do not praise you.* (NKJV)

Then, after explaining how to administer the Lord's Supper, he speaks of how we are to examine ourselves when taking it in 1 Corinthians 11:27–29:

> *27 Therefore whoever eats this bread or drinks this cup of the Lord in an unworthy manner will be guilty of the body and blood of the Lord. 28 But let a man examine himself, and so let him eat of the bread and drink of the cup. 29 For he who eats and drinks in an unworthy manner eats and drinks judgment to himself, not discerning the Lord's body.* (NKJV)

Unfortunately, in today's church, many of us partake of communion without ever living it. Communion is never fully actualized in our lives. Our instructions for communion include reconciling with one another, but just doing it once is not enough; we should live in that reconciliation. I always refer to the fact that we are "not discerning the Lord's body"

(v. 29). When we discern the Lord's body, it makes us sensitive to Calvary, reminding us that Christ died for us while we were yet sinners. It should shine a light on His love for us and His forgiveness of our sin. It should make us mindful that we are to show others the same love, forgiveness, and selflessness that Christ showed to us. This spirit of love and reconciliation should draw us together, not drive us further apart. So how can we continue to take communion over and over again and still be so divided in the church? It is because we do not examine ourselves; we just go through the motions of eating the bread and drinking the juice.

Again, this is why I say that we take communion, but we do not live communion… and this is a problem. What will it take for believers to start examining themselves, obeying the Word of the Lord, and operating in a spirit of unity? In other words, what is it going to take for people to have the disposition of a true believer and go on to maturity? When are we going to grow up?

Here's where the deception creeps in again: I can ask these questions until I'm blue in the face, and people can nod along and say, "Yes, Bishop! How long?" but so many of them are mean, unkind, contentious, and spiritually immature. They live in a state of self-deception. From their perspective, they love God, they are sensitive to Calvary—and that's all that matters. But how can we say that we are sensitive to Calvary and not be sensitive to those we see? John the Beloved said it like this in 1 John 4:20–21:

> *20 If someone says, "I love God," and hates his brother, he is a liar; for he who does not love his brother whom he has seen, how can he love God whom he has not seen? 21 And*

this commandment we have from Him: that he who loves God must love his brother also. (NKJV)

This is not a question easily answered by today's saints. We see the physical bodies of our brothers and sisters, but we fail to discern the body of Christ. How can this be?

Gossiping

One of the primary reasons that people are able to keep chaos, mess, and disorder alive in the church is because, rather than letting things settle, calm, and be put to rest, we breathe life into them through gossip. The Lord told me a while ago to give the people a message: stop talking about it! In the church, we like to gather in our little circles, call up our friends, and talk about what somebody else didn't do. And it doesn't end after one conversation—we keep it going. It might be true that someone said or did something wrong in the church, and yes, they were wrong. However, when others make it a part of their daily discussion, they become just as wrong as the offender. In fact, whenever we feed off of the faults of another person in an attempt to try to feel better about ourselves, we become offenders, too.

The apostle Paul writes in Romans 6:13, "And do not present your members as instruments of unrighteousness to sin, but present yourselves to God as being alive from the dead, and your members as instruments of righteousness to God" (NKJV). Your tongue is considered a "member" and should not be used as an instrument of unrighteousness. Therefore, when your tongue wants to gossip, catch it mid-sentence and say, "You can't talk about Minister so-and-so. You have no right to do anything but bless the Lord at all times."

When we gossip about others, we know what we're doing. We know the person who wronged us is weak. Yet instead of seeing them through the image of God, we enlarge their flaws. Never forget this, saints: no matter how broken we are, we are all created in the image of God. Here's where we fall short: instead of provoking one another to love and good works as the Bible instructs in Hebrews 10:24, we provoke one another to strife and shame. If you know someone is weak—if you see they have a propensity in a certain area—why would you want to stir it up? You should want the strong to bear the infirmities of the weak, and bearing those infirmities does not include gossip. You will never help anyone by talking about them.

The Prevalence of Pride in Keeping People Offended & Odds

The spirit of pride is so subtle that you can walk in it and not even know you're doing it. The Bible describes the serpent in Genesis as being more subtle than any other beast of the field (Genesis 3:1). The devil has always been slick in his tactics. He used his subtlety to bring Adam and Eve down, persuading the woman with the promise, "You'll be as wise as God." What was he appealing to with this statement? Her pride.

Pride gets in the way of people aligning with God's will. The serpent deceived Eve by telling her she'd be wise as God, and that same lie is alive today. Pride makes you unteachable. When leaders try to teach you to love one another, forgive one another, and bear one another's burdens, but you feel that you are exempt from doing so, you are operating under the influence of pride. Pride convinces you that no one can tell you anything or assess you—not even your leader. It deceives you into thinking you're the smartest person in the room and can watch for your own life. But saints, let me tell you, pride is dangerous. Proverbs 16:18 tells us that "Pride goeth before destruction, and an haughty spirit before a fall" (KJV).

I often hear, "But Bishop, they hurt my feelings!" My response? So what. The truth is, they didn't just hurt your feelings—they hurt your pride. That's why you have such a big problem with it. Now, most of the time, I can't tell people this one-on-one because they'll fall out with me. Instead, I have to say these things from the pulpit and hope they get the message.

Someone hurt your pride? Big deal. Who are you, really? How big and important do you feel you are—that no one is allowed to hurt your pride? Other people's pride gets hurt, too. Welcome to the club. And how many people's proud feelings have you hurt? People rarely want to deal with this reality. The irony is, they especially don't want to be challenged about it by their pastor or leader—the very one God assigned to their lives to watch for their souls and help correct their thinking and behavior when they are not aligned with the Word of God.

God forbid anyone get called out in today's church! There is so much pride running rampant that people can hardly listen to the Word with their heart because they're trying to listen with sensitive ears, looking for a reason to be offended by the message. Today's saints, weighed down by pride, wouldn't have survived the first-century church. Go back and read the epistles—Paul called out names! People don't think the pastor should ever personally address anyone in a public forum, whether in worship service, a meeting, or any setting where someone else might hear it. Where did we get this from? I'll tell you: it's straight from our 21st-century mentality, which is steeped in pride. We've been misprogrammed as believers today. That's why the prevailing mindset is, "Don't personalize the Word to me, and don't call me out, Bishop!" People behave however they want, and once they do, they hide behind pride, so that even their leader can't correct them without sparking a clash or risking them walking away from the church.

Our natural predilection is not to be humble, but proud. That's the default. But do you know why you're constantly offended, clashing, and falling out with people? Because of pride. You get all broken up because someone talked about you, and somehow, you feel they diminished the greatness of this big person you believe yourself to be. It's all because of how highly you think of yourself.

I guarantee you, if you operated more out of a spirit of humility and lowliness—with more of a Christlike disposition rather than a carnal, sinful one—your pride wouldn't get hurt as often. And if it did, you wouldn't care as much. Your position would be, "I know their comment might not have painted me in the best light, but who am I? I'm nothing."

You act like no one is supposed to talk about you, but here's the deal—you talk about everybody else. Why do you use this double standard to evaluate how other people treat you, but not how you treat others? Pride. Watch yourself and the spirit of pride, because the enemy will use it to try to take you out!

2

The Disposition of the Believer

A key verse to examine when seeking to understand the disposition of the mature believer is Ephesians 4:23. Let's examine it in several different translations:

> *"And be renewed in the spirit of your mind."* – Ephesians 4:23 (KJV)

> *"And that you be renewed in the spirit of your mind."* – Ephesians 4:23 (New American Standard Bible)

> *"Instead, renew the thinking in your mind by the Spirit."* – Ephesians 4:23 (CEB)

> *"And be continually renewed in the spirit of your mind [having a fresh, untarnished mental and spiritual attitude]."* – Ephesians 4:23 (AMP)

As you can see, each translation reinforces the same truth: it is the Holy Spirit's work to influence and reshape our thinking. Let me ask you: Is the Holy Spirit truly controlling your mind? Is He influencing your thoughts? Are you even open to His influence? These are essential questions for us to consider as we engage in self-reflection about our disposition.

Notice the word "instead" used in the Common English Bible translation of this key scripture. This "instead" points us to a juxtaposition in the text—a challenge to compare how we once thought with how we are called to think now that we have been saved. This nuance highlights the fact that it takes the Holy Spirit to get your thinking together. This is important, because it is your thinking that creates your disposition.

What is a Disposition?

According to the dictionary, a disposition is "a prevailing tendency, mood, or inclination." Do not overlook the word *prevailing* in this definition. A disposition is not something that is momentary or temporary. It is the predominant way you are—the standard, usual way you come across to others. It is your temperamental makeup. Another definition for disposition is "a person's inherent qualities of mind and character." This definition reminds us of another important truth: the believer possesses inherent qualities of mind and character—things that God has placed within us. Some traits are innate, meaning they are already in us at birth. They are in our blood.

For example, I know someone who was called into ministry and used mightily by God. However, long before they fully dedicated their life to Christ, they had a child they didn't know about. Years later, that child came searching for them, and to their surprise, this child—raised without their influence—was a preacher of the Gospel of Jesus Christ. What a testimony to the power of the bloodline! Even though they never had the opportunity to raise that child, the spiritual calling was in the bloodline.

Here's another, more personal example. I've always wanted to play the organ or piano. I even took lessons for a while but never stuck with it. My wife didn't play either, yet both our sons seemingly picked it up out of nowhere. They play beautifully. How is that? Well, on both sides of the family, their grandmothers were accomplished musicians. My wife's mother was the church musician when I arrived in Indianapolis 36 years ago, and my mother was one of the pianists at the Temple on Clinton Street. Though the musical gift skipped us, it was still in the bloodline.

I share these examples to help illustrate that just as we inherit physical and behavioral traits from our earthly family, we also manifest spiritual qualities given by God. When we give our lives to Christ, we become a new creature. That means we are now connected to another bloodline—a *spiritual* bloodline. When the Lord saved us, He gave us a blood transfusion. This means He gave us another disposition, another set of inherent qualities of mind and character.

The blood of Jesus overrides everything you inherited from your natural family tree. Whatever flaws, tendencies, or curses you think you've inherited, the blood of Jesus has the power to break them. Therefore, let's stop dwelling on generational curses. I'm not condemning the term itself, but I am challenging us to shift our focus. Too often, we pick up phrases or ideas in church without fully considering their implications. What we should focus on instead is the fact that the blood of Jesus is greater than anything passed down through your natural bloodline. His blood has the final say in your disposition!

What is your disposition, or temperament? What's your general makeup? Are you melancholic? Angry? Frustrated? When you enter a room, does the atmosphere change for the better or for the worse? Some of us bring a spirit of anger into the atmosphere and then wonder why people are always upset with us. As you ask yourself these self-reflective questions, be bold enough to be honest with yourself.

Our Thinking Determines Our Disposition

When you couple the fact that a disposition can be defined as one's prevailing tendency, mood, or inclination with the fact that our thinking creates our disposition, it stands to reason that the way we think is the reason we act the way we do. You behave the way you do because you think the way you think. This means that if you're mean, it's because you think mean thoughts. If you're angry, it's because you harbor angry thoughts. Knowing that our thoughts strongly influence our attitudes and actions is not new; however, although we know this reality, many people rarely discipline their thinking so that they produce a different disposition.

How many of us can testify that someone did us wrong, and the more we thought about it, the angrier we became? If you can admit to it, you're not going to like this—but your problem is that you aren't thinking correctly. The quickest way to overcome an offense is to let it go, but we don't want to let it go. We hold on to it like a bulldog, revisiting it every time we see the person who wronged us. No wonder so many people are saved but not delivered. We have not done what the apostle Paul wrote in Ephesians 4:23 and allowed the Holy Spirit to renew the spirit of our minds.

You Have the Holy Ghost… but Where's the Transformation?

Consider this example: A person is living in sin. Let's say they're shacking up with someone, and the Lord saves them—but they go right back to the same behavior. Why? Because, even though they received the Spirit, they didn't allow the Spirit to transform their thinking. I'm not among those who say, "If you don't do right, you never had the Holy Ghost." I don't believe that. Instead, I believe that people who have the Holy Ghost often do wrong because they do not allow the Spirit to do His transformative work in their minds.

Whether or not you have the Holy Ghost is not the issue. I'm not questioning this at all. The real question is this: Is the Holy Ghost working in you? Is He transforming you and your mind so that you produce thoughts that manifest in a Christ-like disposition? This is the challenge many believers face. It's not that they don't have the Spirit—it's that they're not allowing Him to work. When He speaks, they ignore

His voice. Instead, we must pray and ask the Holy Ghost to renew the spirit of our thinking so that we can have the disposition of a saint.

Jesus said in John 15:8, "Herein is my Father glorified, that ye bear much fruit; so shall ye be my disciples" (KJV). The same verse reads in the Amplified Bible, "My Father is glorified and honored by this, when you bear much fruit, and prove yourselves to be My [true] disciples." As you read this scripture, ask yourself the question, "How often is my Father honored and glorified by my so-called Christian disposition?" Take a moment to truly consider this. In your last encounter with someone you didn't like—or someone you believed didn't like you—was your Father in Heaven honored and glorified by your thoughts, attitude, and behavior? This is the real standard God wants you to attain, saints of God.

Here's another self-reflective question to ask yourself when you read this scripture: When am I going to prove myself to be one of Christ's disciples? When is the evidence finally going to manifest so that when people look at my life, they see my Christ-like character and behavior and know that I am one of His disciples?

Jesus went on to say in John 15:9-12:

> *I have loved you just as the Father has loved Me; remain in My love [and do not doubt My love for you]. 10 If you keep My commandments and obey My teaching, you will remain in My love, just as I have kept My Father's commandments and remain in His love. 11 I have told you these things so that My joy and delight may be in you, and that your joy may be made full and complete and overflowing.* (KJV)

The Amplified Bible writes verse 11 like this:

> *I have told you these things so that My joy and delight may be in you, and that your joy may be made full and complete and overflowing.*

When you consider this, ask yourself, "Does my Christian disposition bring Jesus joy and delight?" Think about how you act in your home, at your workplace, and in ministry. What do you do—or not do, say—or not say, that Jesus could take joy and delight in?

Ephesians 4:30 says, "Grieve not the Holy Spirit of God, whereby you are sealed unto the day of redemption" (KJV). There's a world of theological depth in this verse. We are sealed—marked, branded, secured—by the Spirit of God until the day of redemption. This sealing is not just a label; it's the Spirit's claim on us, proof that we are His. The AMPC version elaborates on Ephesians 4:30, saying, "And do not grieve the Holy Spirit of God [do not offend or vex or sadden Him], by Whom you were sealed (marked, branded as God's own, secured) for the day of redemption (of final deliverance through Christ from evil and the consequences of sin)."

Here's another self-reflective question to ask yourself as you seek the power of the Spirit to be transformed into a mature believer: "The last time you faced opposition or dealt with an enemy, did you vex, offend, or sadden the Holy Spirit with how you handled it?"

For many people, the answer to this question is not a positive one. The Holy Spirit told me to remind you that He saved you, and He sealed you—but you make Him sad. He saved you, but you don't act like it. You offend Him by how you treat one another, especially your enemies.

Here's why you grieve Him: You've forgotten two critical truths. First, your enemy was created in the image and likeness of God. Second, there was a time when you yourself were an enemy of God, alienated from Him (Romans 5:10). Yet God, in His lovingkindness, drew you to Himself. Even while you were His enemy, He loved you and saved you. He put His Spirit in us, and even after this, we can't manage to talk to one another kindly or get along—walking in love, side by side. Then, after all of our ugliness, God still lets us feel His presence. Even when we grieve Him, God hangs with us. Since you first received Christ, you've done many things you'd be ashamed to admit—but God stuck with you.

Yet when it comes to each other, one wrong move and we're done with our brother or sister. After they offend us or get on our "bad side," we speak nastily or not at all. We distance ourselves, treating people with a long-handled spoon. But God doesn't want all your enemies out of your life—He has them there to teach you how to love them like He loves you. If God deals with us with lovingkindness, why can't we treat one another with the same love?

Don't forget that it was while we were yet sinners that Christ died for us. He didn't wait for us to get it together. He didn't wait for us to act right. And here's the most humbling part: God saw every failure you were ever going to make—every single one—and He still chose to love you and die for you. He still chose you. He still sealed you with His Spirit. This is why we grieve Him: we make a mockery of His love through the way we treat each other.

In John 15, Jesus said, "This is My commandment: that you love one another as I have loved you" (KJV). A commandment, saints, is not optional. And who gave us this commandment? Jesus. He said to love one another in the same manner as He has loved us. This means that loving one another is not a suggestion or a recommendation—it is something He requires us to do.

Let's not grieve the Holy Spirit through our disobedience any longer. Let's love one another as Christ has loved us. That's the standard, and that's His command.

Let me confess something: I have my struggles, too. I'm not perfect, and I need the Holy Ghost to help me rise to this standard, just like you do. I've had to deal with people who vexed my soul—people who knew exactly which buttons to push. Sometimes, I'd get so mad, I could feel it in my fingers! I'll admit, I wanted to tell them, "Get out of my face." But I didn't. Why? Because I know God doesn't like ugly. And I know Jesus calls us to a higher standard, and I'm determined to attain it.

Do Bad Things Keep Happening to You? Check Your Disposition!

When people who are always finding themselves in some mess, conflict, or confusion come to me and ask, "Bishop, why do these things keep happening to me?" I reply, "You need to take a look in the mirror!" Nearly every time these types of people end up in the middle of something, it's rarely the other people—it's them. It's their attitude, temperament, disposition, way of handling things, aggression, strength, stubbornness, need to be right, critical nature, and a whole host of other characteristics that always land them in some kind of mess. The worst part is that while everyone else sees this about them, no one wants to say anything, because they know that this person will go off, get offended, grow defensive, and not listen to anyone else's assessment.

Some people are so fragile that even we, as pastors, have to tiptoe around them. Far too many people simply cannot handle the truth about themselves. In fact, they don't want to hear the truth. This allows them to always play the role of the persecuted one—the victim. It's easier for them to process their bad situations and undesirable outcomes by blaming everyone else. They will tell you that they are spiritual, and yet people don't like them, don't value them, treat them unfairly, and even resent them—and this is why things turned out the way they did. But the reality is, it's not that people resent the God in them; it's the devil they've allowed to work through them that's causing the problems.

One of the ways that we know it to be true that it's the person and not everyone else landing them in these situations is that the same kinds of situations and outcomes follow them everywhere they go. They clash at church. They clash with their spouse or relationship partner. They clash with their parents and siblings. They clash with their coworkers and managers on the job. They clash with everyone. It's not other people landing them in the messes they end up in, it's them. They are the common denominator in all of the messy situations they encounter.

If this sounds like you, let me help you out by giving you some practical advice: It's probably not a good idea to tell your boss off. No matter what they did, how they misunderstood you, or how they treated you, don't go off and give them a piece of your mind. This is just good career advice, and if you heed it, it will help you keep your job. If you're a business owner, it's probably not a good idea to mistreat or go off on your clients. If you do, don't come asking for prayer, saying, "Bishop, the devil is hindering my business!" No—it's you. You're the one driving people away. Instead of asking for prayer against external demons, ask for prayer against the demon in you!

If you're a parent, let me also talk to you for a moment. Some of your children don't want to be around you because you're mean. Your disposition is highly unpleasant. It's not always the devil creating distance and driving your children away—you're doing a good enough job on your own. Your children don't want a sermon every time you talk to them. And let's be real: they've seen your mess, too. They know you're not perfect, so stop pretending you are. They've heard you gossip, criticize the pastor, and tear down others in the church. Then, you tell them to get up and go to church on Sunday, and they're confused—because you've painted everyone there in a negative light. Your children aren't stupid or naïve. They see the inconsistency between what you say and what you do.

They can't say anything, but they're watching. For example, single mothers, they knew when Tom was up in that room with you, and they knew you weren't in there reading the Bible together! Then you want to present yourself as Mother Teresa. Your children are not stupid; they see, know, and understand way more than you think they do. Yes, your children are supposed to respect their parents, but don't think for a moment that they haven't seen through the facade.

Also, parents, not every transgression is sexual in nature. You might not be engaging in sexual immorality, but your children saw you act out in the supermarket. They've heard you gossiping on the phone. They heard you tear down the pastor, criticize the missionary leader, and complain about the people at the camp meeting. They heard you say the pastor "ain't no good" and that "all them folks down there ain't no good." You're always talking about those two sisters you don't like. Your children hear that, too. Then they go to church, and when the Spirit starts moving and the Word convicts them, they're ready to go to the altar. But then they look up and see one of the sisters you've been gossiping about, and their conviction is interrupted. Why? Because your words planted a barrier in their spirit. They can't reconcile your bitterness with the transformation they're being called to. Can you blame them for being confused? You've painted everyone in the church as villains, and yet you expect them to embrace the very community you've criticized. That's a damaging disposition to have in front of your children.

This is why spiritual maturity matters. Some of us need to ask the Lord to help us bridle our tongues. The problem isn't always in what's happening outside of us. Sometimes, the real problem is in what's happening within us. If you've been prone to this disposition, ask God to renew your mind, cleanse your heart, and guard your words—so you don't create stumbling blocks for those closest to you, especially your children.

While I'm on it, let me talk to you if you are a spouse. Wives, your husband doesn't always need to know your conflicts, and husbands, your wife doesn't always need to know yours. Many times, people put their spouses in harm's way over things that could have been handled privately and differently. A wife might have a poor attitude and get told off by someone, and she says to them, "I'm going to tell my husband what you said to me!" However, wives, if your husband is supposed to be saved, what is he going to do about it?

Brothers and sisters, we have to stop operating this way. We are supposed to be saved and Christ-like, and yet we are ready to use our spouses to settle a dispute that we caused with our own bad disposition. You produced a situation that had no business escalating in the first place. Do you really want your spouse coming down to the church to confront another believer? Are we not called to be peacemakers? It's time to allow the Holy Spirit to renew your thinking.

So that no one feels left out, let me also address the single people, especially you younger ones. Many times, your disposition is just too loose and free; it doesn't reflect Christ-like character or the mature disposition of a believer. And you know it—but you give yourself an excuse: "I'm still young, and you shouldn't expect me to act like a fully mature believer yet." However, it is God who puts the expectation on you to go on to maturity once you're saved—not your leader or anyone else. Just because you are younger doesn't mean you can't manifest the disposition of a believer.

Spiritual maturity is not the same as biological maturity. You can be a young person in the things of God and be more mature than a 50- or 60-year-old, if you die to yourself and commit to living your life based on the principles of God and His Word.

That said, single people—stop fornicating! It has become far too acceptable for single people to have "friends with benefits" in the Lord's church. What are you doing traveling with a single man you're not married to when you're saved? Why are you checking into a room together at a convocation? Be discreet. Better yet, stop shacking up and get married! You don't need a big wedding; you need to do what's right. Prioritize sacrifice and holiness over personal gratification.

People say to me, "We're waiting a year for a big wedding." Go on and get married—or stop rubbing on each other. Why won't he marry you? "I've got to get myself together," they say. No, you don't. You're 50 years old, collecting Social Security soon. Stop trying to get everything you want and move forward.

Stop the shacking! Stop acting like you're married when you're not. If you're living together, go on and get married. Then have a blessing ceremony later, and the saints will celebrate with you because you're doing the right thing. Living in an ungodly situation cuts off your blessings. Nothing will work for you until you straighten it out. In the meantime, while you're procrastinating, you're damaging your witness. People are looking at your disposition, and it doesn't appear Christ-like or like you're living a life of sacrifice and self-denial.

Sacrifice means giving up what you could have for something greater. What's the "something greater" here? The greater is the cause of Christ. It is the manifestation of the disposition of the believer that attracts people to Christ and His community of believers in the church. If you get right with God, He won't only bless your life—He will bless others through your life.

I always tell young ladies: You can mess up a good thing by doing it the wrong way. If he loves you, he'll do the right thing. I ask, "How will you know if a man is the one God has for you if you're sleeping with him?" Don't come to me when he leaves you, claiming there's a devil in the church. No—there are two devils: you and him. He wasn't the devil when he was ringing your bell, but now that he's ringing the doorbell next door, you want to meet with the pastor. You'll never know God's will if you won't make sacrifices.

Sacrifice the gratification of physical pleasure and conduct yourself with a disposition of spiritual maturity, single woman of God! You must make a decisive dedication of your body to God, because your body belongs to God—not to you. He bought you with a price. The old saints used to sing, "My body belongs to God, my soul and body belong to God." Songs like that reminded them who they were to God. And because they belonged to God, they didn't just do anything they wanted with their body. They and their bodies were dedicated and devoted to Him.

Let me help you understand how men operate: If he's sleeping with you, he's not likely to marry you—because he's already getting what he wants. When he does decide to marry, do you know who he's going to choose? The woman in the church who conducts herself with the disposition of the believer—who walks in the spirit of love, selflessness, and devotion to Christ.

Thus, I urge you: Prioritize sacrifice and holiness over personal gratification. This is the disposition of the believer.

God's Standard Never Gives You the Green Light to Go Off!

If you consider yourself a mature believer—a "dispositional saint" whose mind has been transformed by the Holy Spirit—you should never allow your circumstances or the actions of others to dictate your behavior. At no point should you find yourself saying, "I've had enough, and I'm about to lose control!" The Lord never gave you permission to blow up, fight, or cuss. Your emotions do not give you the right to violate God's principles or disrespect His people.

You might say, "But Bishop, they kept doing it and pushed me to that point!" This changes nothing about God's expectation that you operate as a mature saint with the disposition of a true believer. God's standard doesn't shift just because your patience is wearing thin. I'm not saying I don't understand the human dynamic—trust me, I've been there. But I've learned to minimize those moments because, at the end of the day, I'm supposed to be saved and operating with the character of Christ.

Allow me to express a thought that might not be very popular with you—especially if you're the kind of saint who always seems to be caught up in some clash or conflict: sometimes, the mistreatment you feel is not real; it's imagined. Sometimes the people you think are against you aren't even thinking about you. They're too preoccupied with their own issues and problems!

I'm reminded of a story that is a prime example of this. I'm reminded of a story that proves the point. I once had a pastor who, unbeknownst to me, thought I wasn't speaking to them. To be honest, they were right—I wasn't trying to speak to them. Do you know how some people are really good folks—sweet people—but they're just... verbose? I'm not talking about gossipers or backbiters. I'm talking about people who just love to talk, and it's hard to have a short conversation with them because they don't know when to stop. This person was like that.

One day, I was in the parking lot and I saw this pastor in my peripheral vision. I knew that if we started talking, I'd be there for a while, and I didn't have the time or the desire to have a long conversation. So, what did I do? I got out of my car, hit the lock button, and ran into the building! Oh yes, I'll admit it: I literally ran! I refused to make eye contact with them. Yes, I may have heard them call my name, but I acted like I didn't hear a thing.

But here's the thing: I also knew the devil was probably whispering lies to that pastor. He was probably saying, "Bishop saw you. He heard you. He just didn't stop to talk to you because he doesn't like you!" But, saints, that wasn't the issue at all. This person was as sweet as apple pie. No, the problem wasn't how nice they were; it was their verbosity... their loquacity. Rather than just saying to themselves, "Bishop was probably busy, rushing in for a meeting," or "Bishop was probably running for the restroom," the enemy twisted it to create offense in this individual. Even though the actions happened the way they did, the mistreatment that the pastor felt was imagined.

The enemy often uses imagined slights to create division among the saints. Don't let the devil deceive you, convincing you that mistreatment exists where it does not. And even when real offenses occur, ask yourself this: "Was my Father in Heaven honored and glorified in my response?" That's the standard.

Do You Really Believe God Can Change Your Contentious Character?

One thing I know to be true is that some of the saints don't even try to change from being their strong, angry, easily offended, contentious, hypersensitive selves that rub people the wrong way—because they feel like, "This is just the way I am." They don't ask the Holy Ghost to keep them. They speak in tongues on Sunday, interpret the Word, and declare, "Help cometh right now!" Yet, when it comes to controlling their temper—where is that help? They believe God for miracles like healing the lame, opening deaf ears, and giving sight to the blind, but they don't believe He can transform their disposition. There's something wrong with this picture.

Have you been challenged with your disposition and gone to the altar for prayer, asking God to miraculously change your character? Do you believe He is able to do so? If you are skeptical about God's ability to change you, perhaps it's because of what's in your heart and mind when you ask Him for this transformation. Imagine this: you're standing at the altar, souls all around you, seeking God for change. But instead of focusing on God, you're having evil thoughts about the sister next to you: "She thinks she's more anointed than me. Let me show her something." Then, after months of harboring that bitterness, you leave the church saying, "Ain't nobody right over there or getting saved over there."

My question to you is, why can't you be delivered from something as simple as your poor attitude or your temper? Do you really believe God is able? Are you still convinced He's in the miracle-working business? If He is, why haven't your prayers worked?

Too many people walk away from their churches every week because of their own poor character and disposition—blaming the church without looking at themselves. You're not supposed to quit a ministry in the church because of a misunderstanding with somebody. Shame on you if you do. When you leave like this, it shows you weren't serving for the Lord in the first place. Whatever God calls you to do, you don't have the right to quit just because you're upset! When you walk away, you're telling God, "When I'm mad, I don't have to obey You." This offends God. When you declare, "Forget those people," Christ's response is, "But they're My people. I died for them." So I ask you, how dare you disregard what God values so highly?

It is up to us not to be like the bulldog, holding on to old ways of thinking. Instead, I challenge you to invite the Holy Spirit to renew your mind, shaping your disposition to reflect the mind of Christ. May Ephesians 4:23 take root in each of us, challenging and changing us for the glory of God.

3

What Spiritual Maturity Looks Like in the Believer's Disposition

At this point, you might be asking, "Bishop, what's the big deal? Why do we need to talk about having the disposition of the believer?" Well, if you are evangelism- and discipleship-minded, the answer should be evident. If we do not get this issue together and help people begin manifesting the disposition of the believer, our churches will be in trouble, and the world will never behold the fullness of the beauty of the body of Christ.

Love is the core aspect of the disposition of the believer. Jesus said in John 13:35, "By this all will know that you are My disciples, if you have love for one another" (NKJV). If our churches are filled with people who refuse to operate with love for one another and reflect the character of Christ, we will be neglecting our responsibility to lift Jesus up before all men. Jesus said, "And I, if I am lifted up from the earth, will draw all peoples to Myself" (John 12:32, NKJV).

When we dominate the church with our carnal attitudes and actions, we are not lifting Christ up—we are lifting ourselves. Lifting ourselves does not draw men to Christ; it repels them. If we are participating in repelling people from the church and turning them off to the idea of having a relationship with Christ—because "If this is the way Christians act, I don't want any part of it!"—do you think God is pleased? I can tell you that He is not. Christ "desires all men to be saved and to come to the knowledge of the truth" (1 Timothy 2:4, NKJV). And if you are interfering with this because you selfishly refuse to go on to become who the Lord intended for you to become when He saved you, you'll have to answer to God for it.

I know there are many who take my words and dismiss them, saying, "Bishop, you have no idea how these people are acting out here. You want me to love them, forgive them, be the bigger person, and act maturely with them—but they are out here acting a fool and cutting up! You just don't know because they don't do it around you!" My response to this is that I don't have to know what people are doing out there. All I need to know is what the Word says, and the Word says that you are to be no longer a babe but to go on to maturity (Hebrews 6:1), love your neighbor as yourself (Mark 12:31), love one another as Christ loved you (John 13:34), consider others more highly than yourself (Philippians 2:3), resolve your offenses in a spiritual manner (Matthew 18:15–17), and forgive others seventy times seven (Matthew 18:22).

A major part of the disposition of the believer is allowing your disposition to be driven by the Word of God—not by your feelings, your experiences, or your subjective opinions. There is no, "I would act kinder and more maturely, but…" There are no excuses or conditions to obeying the Word of God. If the Bible says to do it, we are to do it—no matter what. There are no workarounds for obeying the way God tells us to operate.

Think about it: if everyone in the body of Christ were allowed to find a reason to be exempt from God's expectation of our disposition, no one in the church would feel the need to reflect Christ in their disposition. No one would be compelled to go on to maturity and grow up!

What Does the Disposition of a Mature Believer Look Like?

As you've likely come to understand by now, a mature believer isn't defined solely by their scriptural knowledge or longevity in the faith, but by the consistency of their Christ-like conduct in everyday life. Spiritual maturity shows up in how we handle conflict, how we interact with others, and whether our disposition truly mirrors the heart of Christ. Let's take a look at some practical ways this kind of maturity takes shape in the life of the believer.

Strengthening the Brethren

One of my favorite characteristics of what the disposition of a mature believer looks like comes from something that Jesus said to Peter in Luke 22:31-32:

> *31 And the Lord said, "Simon, Simon! Indeed, Satan has asked for you, that he may sift you as wheat. 32 But I have prayed for you, that your faith should not fail; and when you have returned to Me, strengthen your brethren."* (NKJV)

It's that part at the end that reveals a key trait of the mature believer: after you go through some things, you use the lessons you've learned, your experiences, and your testimony to strengthen others. Ask yourself, "Am I a strengthener of others, or am I the opposite—a detractor or a weakener?" Do you rejoice in the failings of others, or are you sincerely moved to come alongside them and offer spiritual support and help? When you have the opportunity to be a source of strength, do you operate in that—or do you see someone in need and look the other way because you've got your own spiritual life, your own schedule, and your own struggles to tend to?

I'd suggest that a whole lot of believers just look the other way. We don't have many people willing to help others who are struggling in the church today.

Being Led by God's Word, Not Emotions

Ask yourself: What determines how I behave day to day? What influences how I respond when others rub me the wrong way? How do I decide how to react when someone says something reckless to me—or about me? What determines what my face looks like when I walk into the house of God? How would people describe my disposition the last time I was at a ministry meeting or event—and what contributed to that? What was the reason my disposition was that way?"

If your answer to any of these questions has anything to do with how you were feeling at the time, what was on your mind, or simply "that's just how I am… I believe in keeping it real," you have some reflecting to do.

One of the main reasons we tend to conduct ourselves contrary to the character of Christ is because we don't allow Calvary or Christ to inform us of how we are to behave. How you behave should always be birthed out of a conscious decision to function a certain way—because it is how the Bible tells you to function. Whether you feel it or not. Whether it matches your natural tendencies or not.

Preferring Others Over Ourselves

I believe many of Jesus' teachings in the Sermon on the Mount ought to be taken primarily literally. For example, in Matthew 5:21–22a, He said:

> 21 *"You have heard that it was said to those of old, 'You shall not murder, and whoever murders will be in danger of the judgment.' 22 But I say to you that whoever is angry with his brother without a cause shall be in danger of the judgment"* (NKJV).

Do you get angry with your brother for silly reasons—reasons that are really only differences in opinion and not true grounds for anger or for despising them in your heart?

He said in Matthew 5:38-39:

> 38 *"You have heard that it was said, 'An eye for an eye and a tooth for a tooth.' 39 But I tell you not to resist an evil person. But whoever slaps you on your right cheek, turn the other to him also."* (NKJV)

When someone slaps you on the cheek or offends you, do you rise up and go off on them, prepare to curse them out, or even get ready to physically fight them? Or do you turn the other cheek and say, "Is there anything else I need to bring before the Lord so He can transform me in that area?"

Jesus said in Matthew 5:41-42:

> 41 *"And whoever compels you to go one mile, go with him two. 42 Give to him who asks you, and from him who wants to borrow from you do not turn away."* (NKJV)

Do you go the extra mile for your brother? Are you generous with your brothers and sisters—especially when you've been blessed with excess and they're clearly in need?

From what I have observed and experienced, rarely do saints live this way. We really don't consider or prefer our brothers or sisters before ourselves. We aren't truly willing to be the living sacrifice that the apostle Paul calls us to be in Romans 12:1:

> *I beseech you therefore, brethren, by the mercies of God, that you present your bodies a living sacrifice, holy, acceptable to God, which is your reasonable service.* (NKJV)

Pay close attention to the word "sacrifice" that appears here and the message it is intended to convey. There's no such thing as sacrificing an animal that's alive. In order to be a living sacrifice, we have to die to ourselves. If we don't truly die in order to present ourselves as that living sacrifice, all we'll do is creep off the altar when we grow tired of making the sacrifice.

Seeing & Trying to Understand Others

There was a movie that was popular several years ago named *Avatar*. There was a line in the movie that really struck me—and even to this day, I think of it often. One of the characters asked the question, "Do you see me?" If you've never seen the movie, the gist of it was that through some scientific avatar program, human beings on earth were able to be matched to the bodies of blue-skinned, humanoid beings, which they remotely controlled. These avatars operated in another world—a fictional planet called Pandora. When they were on Pandora, they did not see each other for the human beings they really were on earth; all they saw was each other's avatar.

It was during one moving moment in the movie that one of the avatars asked another avatar—whom they knew in real life back on earth—"Do you see me?" They were essentially asking the other person, "Do you see me for who I really am underneath this blue body that I'm wearing? Do you see the real me—my humanity?"

I give this example because I do not believe we truly see one another in the church in terms of our humanity. We do not recognize the needs our brothers or sisters may have. We don't see that they have the same fears and concerns as us—that they love their children and families like us, that they carry their own fair share of insecurities and struggles just like us, or that they're on their Christian journey, striving and stumbling just like us.

We don't take the time to see one another. Instead, we take each other at face value and never look beyond the surface. They have feelings, too, and those feelings get hurt when we are unkind or ignore them. They need to connect with others on a deeper level, and they feel rejected when we stick to our little cliques rather than take interest in them or even speak to them. They need to be understood and accepted—not left to fend for themselves and "figure it out" like you did when you joined the ministry.

When we understand this, we're more likely to operate with empathy toward the saints, rather than treating them like they don't matter or like they are disposable. The way we view and treat one another directly shapes the proper disposition of the saint.

Restoring Rather Than Exposing Saints Who Stumble

So, what should you do if you encounter a brother or sister who has either revealed some sanctification issues or whose holiness facade has developed some holes in it so that you see some of the issues they are having? You should heed Paul's instructions in Galatians 6:1-3:

> *Brethren, if a man is overtaken in any trespass, you who are spiritual restore such a one in a spirit of gentleness, considering yourself lest you also be tempted. 2 Bear one another's burdens, and so fulfill the law of Christ. 3 For if anyone thinks himself to be something, when he is nothing, he deceives himself.* (NKJV)

This is how people with the disposition of the believer operate. They respond to learning about someone's trespasses with spiritual discernment—not judgment, not gossip, and not criticism. They don't run to their circle or clique and say, "Listen, we need to pray for our brother or sister because I just learned something really juicy about their business, and I have to tell you all about it before we pray!" No, people who have a spiritual disposition restore their brother or sister gently—without judgment or condemnation. They encourage them, pray for them, and cover them rather than exposing them. Why? Not only because they are spiritual, but because they know that next time, it could be them. They themselves could be overtaken in a trespass, and they'll need to believe God will send someone to help them through it—with spirituality and confidentiality. This is the way we are to bear one another's burdens—with care, concern, compassion, and understanding.

Now, I have to tell you the truth. Based on what I've observed in the church, we don't have many spiritual people who can help their brothers and sisters be restored, because most of them lack true empathy and compassion. Even though Paul says, "considering yourself," which means to be introspective, few people in the church truly do this. Self-reflection—or introspection—is a critical part of a spiritual person's life, because without it, they can easily fall into self-righteousness. And we have a lot of self-righteous people in our churches.

One thing Christ decried the most was self-righteousness. He was adamantly opposed to it. And here's the strangest thing about it: oftentimes, the people in church who appear the most holy on the outside are the most self-righteous on the inside. They never truly took on the disposition of the believer, which is a mindset to spiritually restore—in the spirit of love, kindness, and grace. We are the hands of Christ in this world to restore, so we must get on our job and take it seriously.

I believe strongly in this. I used to preach for the late Bishop McMurray, and one year, during one of his conferences I preached, his theme was "Restore, Repair, Recover." It resonated with me so deeply that when I was preparing the theme for the new year at my own church, I decided to use it as well. We must keep this at the forefront of our lives as believers—because this is part of the disposition that God expects all believers to have.

Some people believe that being sensitive to the needs of others, or spiritually restoring those in need of ministry, is something "certain people" or "other people" are responsible for—not them. They feel it isn't their personality or responsibility. "That's not really my thing. Let the leaders do it—that's what they're there for," they say.

If you've ever said this—or anything even remotely close to it—you need to know that this aspect of the believer's disposition is something every believer should possess. When you were born again, you became a new creation—and that should have resulted in you developing a new disposition: the disposition of the believer, driven by the Holy Spirit.

Thus, we should all be able to spiritually restore others and reconcile people to Christ when they're distant from Him—whether because they are unsaved or have drifted due to sanctification issues. The apostle Paul said in 2 Corinthians 5:17–18:

Therefore, if anyone is in Christ, he is a new creation; old things have passed away; behold, all things have become new. Now all things are of God, who has reconciled us to Himself through Jesus Christ, and has given us the ministry of reconciliation. (NKJV)

Paul was referring to himself, but by association, this applies to all believers. We all have the ministry of reconciliation—reconnecting people to Christ.

Doing Good to Those Who Wrong You

Those who are spiritually mature do not allow the poor treatment and disrespect of others to motivate them to act the same way. Instead, regardless of how they are treated or how the other person makes them feel, they make a conscious choice to conduct themselves in the manner the Bible instructs—knowing that God will take care of them. Romans 12:20 says, "Therefore if thine enemy hunger, feed him; if he thirst, give him drink: for in so doing thou shalt heap coals of fire on his head" (KJV).

This scripture encapsulates the inherent qualities of mind and character that belong to believers. We are called to love those who oppose us—even while they are opposing us.

You will notice that it does not tell you to let your enemy starve; it tells you to feed him. If he's thirsty, give him a drink—not that old, flat soda that's been in the back of your fridge for weeks, but something fresh. Why? "For in so doing thou shalt heap coals of fire on his head." I know this is counterintuitive for most of us as human beings; we naturally think of responding the opposite way to an enemy. But this is where a transformed mind comes in. We will only operate this way if we allow our natural minds to be changed—so that we function with the mind of Christ.

Many saints think that heaping coals of fire on someone's head is about getting back at them, but that's not what the scripture is teaching. Too often, we do the right thing outwardly, but our hearts betray us. "I'll feed him, but I'm only doing it to heap those coals of fire on him. I want him to burn!" That's not God's way. You can do the right thing, but if your spirit is wrong, it's still sin. You can't serve someone out of vengeance and call it love. You can't give with a self-righteous attitude and expect God to approve. The truth is, doing the right thing with the wrong spirit doesn't make you as 'saved' as you think you are.

In scripture, fire purifies. Think about these words in Job 23:10: "When He hath tried me, I shall come forth as gold" (KJV). Fire refines. This is the work God wants to do—not just in you, but in your enemy. When your enemy mistreats you, you are to do good to them so that the Lord can rid them of their evil—not so you can 'get even.' God's intention is to make your enemy better, not to destroy them.

What is a practical example of Romans 12:20? There are many ways to apply it, but keep in mind that you must apply it not out of mere obligation, but out of love. Let's say, for example, you have an enemy in the workplace—someone who mistreats you, always tries to make you look bad, undermines you, and really gets on your nerves. Tomorrow morning, on your way to work, buy them some donuts and place them on their desk. Swallow your pride, and say to them, "I love you." Here's the part where many of us struggle: do it without expecting anything in return. Too often, we give "contingent apologies." We say, "I'm sorry," but if the other person doesn't reciprocate, we stay mad. That kind of apology isn't genuine. A true apology lets go of pride and anger. This is what doing good to those who wrong you looks like in action.

Doing good to those who wrong you also looks like not being petty with those who are petty with you. I often hear people say, "Bishop, they didn't speak to me, so why am I supposed to speak to them?" After hearing this for so long, I just shake my head and think, Are you a child? If they didn't speak to you, you speak to them. And let me add this: when you speak, don't do it to poke at them. In other words, don't speak just to make a point. Don't speak to say, "See there, I knew they weren't going to speak back to me," just so you can call someone afterward and say, "I spoke to them, and they didn't speak back." There's no victory in that.

I'm reminded of the story of a woman who had a fight with her husband one morning. Harsh words were exchanged, and he walked out the door. Later that day, he passed away at work. Needless to say, she regretted those final words for the rest of her life. The lesson in this story is that one day, your loved one might walk out the door and not come back. Therefore, watch how you treat one another. If they don't apologize to you, don't worry about it. Do what you're supposed to do. And if someone apologizes to you, be gracious. Truly forgive others, even if they've done you wrong.

Let's also learn a lesson from Job. The Bible tells us in Job 1:5:

> *And it was so, when the days of their feasting were gone about, that Job sent and sanctified them, and rose up early*

> *in the morning, and offered burnt offerings according to the number of them all: for Job said, It may be that my sons have sinned, and cursed God in their hearts.* (KJV)

Job was spiritually sensitive enough to offer sacrifices for his children—just in case they sinned. He was proactively saying, "I'm sorry" to God without any evidence that wrong had even been done. Why? Because it was important that if there was any chance his sons had offended God, he wanted to make amends. If Job could humble himself this way, so can we.

Here's what that looks like in practice: You simply say to others, "If I did something to offend you, I'm sorry." It costs you absolutely nothing to say this—except your pride. And that's a small price to pay for peace and being in the will of God. This, my friends, is the standard of a Christian.

Want True Transformation? Don't Get Distracted by Externals

Each of these characteristics helps us understand what the disposition of a mature believer looks like. If you set your sights on them and pray that the Spirit would transform your thinking and help you embrace them as a part of how you operate, you'll be well on your way to maturity.

Whatever you do, don't get caught up majoring in minors and minoring in majors in your quest to function as a mature believer. One of the reasons we become so focused on other people in the church is because it's easier to focus outward than to face the fact that God is calling us to be one way, but we are living another. Our focus should be less external and more internal.

Most of the external things we obsess over aren't even central to God's standards; the enemy simply diverts our attention away from ourselves and onto these things so that we neglect becoming all that God has called us to be. But if you focus on your own internal transformation and the daily manifestation of Christ's character, God will take care of the externals. The external things are His business—not yours, anyway.

For example, we get hung up on surface-level issues like whether someone wears an earring or a bracelet in church, but we overlook the weightier matters of the faith. God's standard is not about how many bracelets or earrings you're wearing; it's about the condition of your heart. He isn't worried about the lipstick on your lips. It's not about the length of your shirt sleeve or the outward things we love to critique. He's looking to see if you're feeding your hungry enemy and giving drink to the thirsty. What if the entirety of our sainthood were measured by how we responded to our enemies—not by how long your dress is, but by how you treat those who mistreat you? That is the true standard.

The real test is: Can you treat your enemy right while they're still treating you wrong? Can you respond with love even when there's no positive return on your kindness? We often look for an immediate response, and when we don't get it, we're quick to release ourselves from the obligation to do right. But treating people right, regardless of their response, is what it truly means to live up to God's high standard.

4

Empathy: The Key Ingredient of the Mature Believer's Disposition

Because we do not strive to embrace the proper disposition of the saints, we often come across as uncaring, unfriendly, and even cold or selfish. It's not uncommon for people to describe members of a church as lacking empathy, which the dictionary defines as "the action of understanding, being aware of, being sensitive to, and vicariously experiencing the feelings, thoughts, and experience of another." However, having empathy for others is a clear expectation that God has for us.

Whenever I think of a biblical example of empathy, my mind goes back to the parable of the Good Samaritan—told by Jesus to a lawyer who had asked Him what he needed to do to inherit eternal life. The parable appears in Luke 10:30–37:

> *30 Then Jesus answered and said: "A certain man went down from Jerusalem to Jericho, and fell among thieves, who stripped him of his clothing, wounded him, and departed, leaving him half dead. 31 Now by chance a certain priest came down that road. And when he saw him, he passed by on the other side. 32 Likewise a Levite, when he arrived at the place, came and looked, and passed by on the other side. 33 But a certain Samaritan, as he journeyed, came where he was. And when he saw him, he had compassion. 34 So he went to him and bandaged his wounds, pouring on oil and wine; and he set him on his own animal, brought him to an inn, and took care of him. 35 On the next day, [j]when he departed, he took out two denarii, gave them to the innkeeper, and said to him, 'Take care of him; and whatever more you spend, when I come again, I will repay you.' 36 So which of these three do you think was neighbor to him who fell among the thieves?" 37 And he said, "He who showed mercy on him." Then Jesus said to him, "Go and do likewise."* NKJV

The priest and the Levite—religious Jews we would expect to stop and help their neighbor—lacked empathy. They left the wounded man lying half-dead in the road. However, the Good Samaritan, who by cultural standards would have been the least likely to help a Jewish man, went to where the man was and helped him. He had compassion and took care of his needs, not only in that moment, but for the immediate future as well. He showed empathy!

Remember, Jesus told this story in response to someone asking how to inherit eternal life—and His answer was a story about demonstrating empathy. Considering this, how do you think God feels about our lack of empathy in the church, when this should be an essential part of the believer's disposition?

We know that in the self-centered busyness of our lives, we often fail to take the time to "bear ye one another's burdens," as Scripture instructs us in Galatians 6:2 (KJV). And that's a problem—because without empathy, we cannot reflect the heart of Christ.

Empathy is not just necessary for helping and ministering to others; empathy is essential for truly understanding them. Stephen Covey, author of the bestselling book *The 7 Habits of Highly Effective People*, listed as his fifth habit: "Seek first to understand, then to be understood." With this, he emphasized the importance of listening carefully to others to grasp what they're really saying, where they're coming from, and the true message they're trying to communicate—before we start speaking in our own defense. The essence of what he was promoting was empathy, which helps us connect with people and build stronger relationships. Highly effective people operate with empathy. How much more should we, the people of God, do the same?

Think about how you give yourself grace because you understand your own flaws and imperfections and how they affect your behavior. Think about how, when you get snappy or impatient with someone—or you say or do the wrong thing—you excuse yourself because you were really hungry, you just got bad news about a family member, you had a hard day at work, you're concerned about your child, you received a troubling diagnosis, you're battling financial pressure, anxiety, depression, or even some form of abuse behind the scenes. You understand yourself, so you don't beat yourself up. You forgive yourself. You extend grace to yourself. Well, *that's what empathy looks like* when you're relating to your brothers and sisters in Christ.

Sometimes, you have to look beyond the sin in someone else and ask, "What made them like this?" or "What pain might have caused them to act this way?" Go deeper. Instead of judging them as a bad person, ask God to help you understand the bad *day* or *season* that may be shaping their behavior. Most of the time, if they say or do the wrong thing to you, it has nothing to do with you. They're just reacting to the pressures of what they're dealing with behind the scenes. So, give them the benefit of the doubt. Extend them grace. And then *pray and intercede* for them.

I remember a sister in my church years ago who had her share of run-ins with others. People said she had a bad attitude. They didn't have much positive to say about her. But I knew she was trying. She was putting in the effort and hanging in there. One day, she sat down and told me her story. As it turns out, when she was a little girl, she had a traumatic childhood. Her mother would be turning tricks with men in one room—and she had her daughter, this young lady, also turning tricks in another. I had pastored her for years before she ever felt safe enough to tell me this, and when she did, it nearly brought me to tears. It became my *a-ha* moment as her pastor. When I finally understood the layers of trauma, rejection, and pain she carried, I saw how it had shaped the distanced, insecure, no-nonsense adult others misjudged. She had been traumatized. Now, I'm not justifying meanness in church, but a mature believer's disposition would respond not with judgment, but with grace. They'd say, "I wonder why she is the way she is. I know there must be something deeper going on. I won't take her behavior personally. I'll pray for her. Maybe I'll even try to connect with her outside of service to see how I can minister to her." That's the kind of empathy and understanding that should define the believer's disposition—not criticism, gossip, or dismissal.

Because I'm a bishop who's been doing ministry for decades, I've heard many confidential stories that most church members will never know. Stories of abuse. Incest. Infidelity. Secret struggles. Silent suffering. And I'm sure many other pastors and leaders have the same kind of insight. You may never know the stories we've heard. And you don't need to. All you need is the spiritual sensitivity to understand that *99% of the time, people's behavior has a backstory*. That's why, when a church leader says, "Be kind. Love one another. Forgive. Seek to understand," you shouldn't push back or second guess it—you should just obey. Because you're not obeying them; you're obeying the Word of God. And obeying the Word is obedience to God Himself.

I can't stress this enough: Empathy is a key characteristic in the disposition of the believer. Why? Because in the church, we love to holler about holiness—but the greatest threat to true holiness is the lack of empathy. In today's church, we judge and dismiss people with shocking ease. Offend someone once, and they'll write you off permanently. But how many times have we offended Christ? And how many times has *He* forgiven us—even when we repeat the same sin intentionally?

We don't take the time to truly know one another. Instead, we immediately gravitate toward people who look like us, think like us, and act like us. We create inner circles and keep everyone else at a distance. We barely talk to people outside of our "crew" or our "circle."

Even worse, we've grown desensitized. People can go missing from service for weeks, and we won't even notice—let alone check on them—and that's tragic. Even more tragic? Some of us don't even know they were missing.

Sometimes in the church, we have to go the extra mile to see through the eyes of others and truly understand their perspective. After all, this is exactly what Christ did for us. The reason He is able to succor and help us is because He first took the time to understand us. And the reason He understood us is because He allowed Himself to be placed in our position.

I recall an incident when I had two families in my church that reached an impasse. Both had youth involved in a particular situation; one youth had done something to the other, and now their families were in conflict. The family of the youth who had been violated wanted to go after the other youth— and, as you can imagine, those parents weren't having it. So of course, the families came to me, their pastor.

My biggest challenge in the situation was that the parents of the offended youth weren't willing to consider things through the lens of the other parents. Did they really expect the other parents to hand their child over to be destroyed? I encouraged them to try to see it through the eyes of the parents whose child was accused. Why did they assume those parents wouldn't defend their child—right or wrong—just as fiercely as they were defending their own?

The truth is, they weren't mature enough to see it. They were unwilling to step outside their pain to try and understand how challenging the situation was for the other family—even though that child was in the wrong.

Over the years, I've actually lost some individuals from my church because of seasoned saints who lacked empathy. In one case, people were put out of the church who could have been salvaged. But I'll admit—I'm human. In that moment, I was guilty of what another leader in a previous story was guilty of: not wanting to look too soft on unholiness.

In that situation, one of my senior members got wind of the matter and jumped ahead of me. They ran their mouth through the entire church. They talked to everybody about it. Why they would do that, I'll never fully understand—but it forced me into a corner. Once the whole church knew what had happened, I couldn't deal with the matter privately anymore. I couldn't help those individuals the way I wanted to. I couldn't protect or cover them. Instead, I had to ask them to leave.

And that never should have happened. The whole thing could have been handled with grace—if only people had been led by the Spirit of God, not by their thirst for exposing and condemning someone. That senior member was just out for blood. I was deeply disappointed in them.

When I asked myself why they would do something like that, I came to one simple realization: they lacked the capacity for empathy.

Saints, don't tie your pastor's hands. Don't take away his ability to help people by putting him in impossible positions. Because one day, it might be your child who needs to be covered and restored. And one day, it might even be you.

5

Still a Babe After Years of Salvation? Something's Wrong!

It's time for us to set the bar higher for the people of God when it comes to what we expect from believers in the church. Remaining a babe in Christ long term can no longer be an option. Growing more and more mature the longer we walk with God must become the standard and expectation.

After we are saved, the expectation is that we become more and more like Christ—reflecting more of who He is than who we naturally are. But sadly, this doesn't seem to be happening in many churches today. Instead, people claim to have experienced salvation, but years later, they're still behaving the same way they did before they got saved. Some are like these five years into their journey, while others are 20 years in—and still not manifesting the character of Christ. How long is it going to take? What is it going to take to get them to this point?

We talk about having the mind of Christ and operating in a Christ-like manner, with a new nature driven by the fruit of the Spirit—but for many, it's just talk. It's all conversation and no manifestation. There are people who have been in church a long time who are still as mean, uncooperative, selfish, or standoffish as they were from day one. I often want to ask them, "Didn't you say you gave your life to Christ? Didn't you say you got saved?" If that's true, why is there no fruit? Why is there no visible difference in your life all these years later—because sir, or ma'am, you are not looking anything like Christ.

What Does the Disposition of a Babe in Christ Look Like?

Have you ever seen one of those extreme makeover shows on TV where people go through complete transformations? You see someone who starts off looking undesirable, and then they look completely different after they're renewed. That's what God does for us when He saves us—He transforms us into something new, restoring His image within us. As a result, it stands to reason that we should look different after we are saved than we did before we were saved, right?

Unfortunately, that's not the case for many of the saints. If they didn't explicitly tell us they had a supernatural experience at salvation—where they were made a new creation in Christ—we would never know! Why? Because they look exactly the same. Who they are and how they come across after salvation is no different than before. In other words, there's no detectable change. The only difference might be that now, they wear church clothes on Sundays. Other than that, there's no visible evidence in their attitude, actions, or disposition that indicates they've had an encounter with God.

These are saints who have remained babes in Christ. Let's take a moment to examine what babes look like.

Out-of-control Emotions

Babes are self-centered, impulsive, and driven by their appetites. They cry, scream, and throw tantrums to get what they want because they have not fully developed their communication skills or learned how to manage their emotions. I hate to say it, but people in the church who have remained in the babe stage after so many years act the same way. Their emotions are out of control. They are constantly engaged in conflict or clashing with others, and instead of resolving issues spiritually—by going to their brother or sister as the Scripture tells us to do in Matthew 18:15–17—they go off and throw adult tantrums, wreaking havoc and causing chaos in the church. They lack the maturity that comes with developing the disposition of the believer. Something's got to change.

Saints driven by their impulses allow their feelings to dictate their actions rather than submitting their emotions to the guidance of the Holy Spirit. Just as a child might stomp their feet when they don't get their way, immature believers tend to lash out—whether through gossip, angry outbursts, or passive-aggressive behavior—when they are offended or feel overlooked or undervalued. They might even get on social media to air their grievances instead of going directly to their brother or sister, as Jesus instructed in Matthew 18:15–17. This creates division rather than unity and undermines the spiritual health of the church.

If this is how you tend to feel and operate, ask the Holy Spirit to teach you how to process your emotions prayerfully, seeking wisdom and resolution in a Christ-like manner. Ask Him to help you manifest aspects of the fruit of the Spirit—such as self-control and gentleness—and to help you prioritize peace and reconciliation over your own desires. Only then will others be able to see that you're stepping into the maturity that reflects the character of Christ.

Lack of Concern for Brothers and Sisters

Those who remain babes in Christ are also those who have not experienced the kind of growth and transformation necessary to "discern the body of Christ," as the apostle Paul writes in 1 Corinthians 11:29, "For he who eats and drinks in an unworthy manner eats and drinks judgment to himself, not discerning the Lord's body" (NKJV).

As a result, they don't take the time to reflect on and appreciate the fact that Christ died for their sin—offering grace, mercy, and forgiveness—and that He expects us to exemplify the same character, extending grace, mercy, and forgiveness to others. Only mature believers can translate the love they've received from Christ into the love they show to others. In doing so, they see beyond the surface of their brothers and sisters and develop a sensitivity that makes them more inclined to empathize When you don't feel concern for your brothers and sisters in Christ—to the point that you're not willing to go out of your way to help them or at least sincerely pray for them—this is a clear indication that you are suffering from arrested growth and spiritual immaturity.

Let me say it another way: you are not a mature believer in Christ. How much you truly love and care for your brothers and sisters is a strong indicator of where you are on your spiritual journey. It gives a clear picture of your level of maturity in Christ.

You might say, "Well, it's not that serious. I'm fine with that!" But Christ is not. In refusing to grow up in the things of God—especially after spending years claiming to walk with Him—you have failed to become what you are called to be in Christ.

Inconsistency in the Things of God

A lack of consistency in the things of God and in your church is also an indicator that you are likely still a babe in Christ. When you commit to reading your Bible, praying, and spending time in devotion, how long does that resolution actually last? Is it short-lived? When you join a ministry team or auxiliary at church, are you committed long-term, or do you float in and out depending on how much commitment and sacrifice are required?

Would your leader—and those who work with you in ministry—say you are consistent, reliable, and dependable? Or do they know that your involvement on any ministry team, project, or task is likely going to be temporary—because you're the kind of person who shows up for a season, then disappears? Are you known in your church for starting but not finishing? For quitting before the assignment is completed? Would others describe you as someone who hands back a task or commitment unfinished—along with a list of excuses about how other people or circumstances kept you from getting the job done?

If any of these scenarios describe you, you're inconsistent—and you are operating like a babe.

Inability to Receive Correction

Another sign of spiritual immaturity is an inability to receive correction. A leader can often discern your level of maturity simply by how you respond to correction. Can you receive an open rebuke without considering resigning from your ministry post—or even leaving the church altogether? Does being corrected—whether you're right or wrong—leave you angry, resentful, or bitter toward those who corrected you, especially your leader? Do you trust your leader's spiritual assessment of you over your own self-assessment?

If you cannot trust the evaluation of the one who watches over your soul—and refuse to submit to godly correction—then you are operating at the level of a babe in Christ.

A mature believer understands that correction, though uncomfortable, is a necessary part of growth and spiritual refinement. It is an opportunity to reflect, learn, and grow—not an attack. When you are unable to receive correction, you are not only stunting your spiritual development—you are rejecting the very process God uses to shape you into His image.

Hebrews 12:6 reminds us that "the Lord disciplines the one He loves" (NIV), and those who resist correction from their leaders are often resisting the Lord's hand in their lives.

A clear sign that you are growing from babe to mature believer is seen in your humility—your willingness to admit you don't have all the answers and that God, through your spiritual leaders, may reveal blind spots you simply cannot see. If pride or defensiveness drives your response to correction, you will remain stuck in spiritual immaturity—never fully benefiting from the transformative power of discipline God intends for your life.

Easily Conforming to Worldly Influences

Babes in Christ tend to mold their behavior not based on what the Word says, but based on what other people will think of them. External influences dictate how they live, think, and dress—their hairstyle, where they go, how they spend their money, and more. They let fashion designers and influencers determine what's "in" and what's "out," and they follow the trends—even if it means tightening their clothes and showing more skin.

They also conform in the quality of how they present themselves publicly. Back in the day, ladies wouldn't dare step off the bus with rollers in their hair—mothers wouldn't allow it. But today, many young ladies have shifted, conforming to what the world deems acceptable. It no longer matters to them that they're representing Christ and His church, so they should be presentable; instead, they look around, see what others are doing, and conform to the world and do it, too.

Babes feel they have to be like the world—or others in the world—in order to be accepted. I tell them, instead of conforming, dare to be different and unique, just as God made you to be! As long as you're trying to mimic others and follow the trends, you'll never truly succeed. Times may change, but God's values remain the same. Clothing and hairstyles evolve, but the values of believers should remain rooted in Scripture. You can adapt to changing styles without conforming to the world or compromising your identity in Christ.

Conforming to a worldly mindset—like embracing a competitive spirit—can kill your spiritual life. God didn't call you to keep up with others; He called you to follow Him. Opportunities to conform to the world will always come—but it is the babes in Christ who are most vulnerable to them.

For example, if you're a gifted and talented musician who hasn't matured in the things of God, you must be cautious about trying to fit in with the gospel music world—because not everyone in gospel music is a gospel person. There will be promoters you'll need to politely turn down. They might offer you a platform—but at what cost? They could rob you of the image of God in your life. More isn't always better. "What does it profit a man to gain the whole world and lose his soul?" The devil has platforms, too—and not every opportunity is from God.

That's why you need to pray and use discernment before accepting what's offered to you. Ask yourself, "What is this going to cost me?" Everything the devil offers comes with strings attached. Be careful about allowing your inclinations to conform to the world and what it offers—especially if you know you haven't matured in Christ. If you continue spending your time conforming to others' expectations, you'll ultimately lose sight of God's plan for your life.

Competing with Others

Babes in Christ often get caught up in how they look—and this prideful obsession drives them to compete in ways that make them appear better than their brothers and sisters in Christ. They dwell in superficiality rather than becoming comfortable with authenticity. To them, externals matter more than spiritual substance. In fact, they spend so much energy managing how people perceive them outwardly that they don't leave room for the Holy Spirit to work on them inwardly.

When people are spiritually immature, they chase opportunities to do what others are doing—but only to one-up the competition. For example, you might've seen your friend and their family out in the park among the autumn trees, so you ran out there to take pictures too, just to show, "Me and my family go to the autumn trees, too!" Now you've got hay fever and are suffering from an allergy attack so bad you have to miss church or work! I'm not saying there's anything wrong with enjoying fall, apple cider, or the outdoors—if that's authentically you. But if it's not, don't force it just to impress people. Don't showcase a version of your life just to prove you're doing it better.

Spiritually immature parents do this as well. Everyone is trying to outdo each other using their children. You see someone else's child graduate from college, and now you're beating yourself up because yours didn't go to school. But maybe God didn't design your children to take that route! Stop competing with other parents—it only creates frustration in your home and unnecessary pressure on your children.

Some parents tear down their children's self-image because they want them to be like someone else's kids. But here's where we often go wrong: we try to create our children in our image instead of letting God shape them. Your job is to provide knowledge and opportunity, but you must let God order their steps. Show them doors—A, B, and C—and then encourage them to go through the one God leads them to. If they choose a door you didn't expect, affirm them anyway. Say, "I'm proud of you." Because God has a unique plan for everyone. So babe in Christ, *stop it* with the competition!

Are Carnality, Comfort & Convenience Keeping You Stuck in the Babe Stage?

Something has crept into the church, convincing people they are okay and in the will of God even though they don't exhibit any change after years of being in the things of God. I believe one of the greatest threats to spiritual growth today is the spirit of deception. People are convinced they are something in God and somewhere in God that they are not. There is nothing about their lives that others can look at and say, "She must have a real relationship with God," or "He must be born again—he doesn't act like everybody else or respond like most people would in difficult situations."

Furthermore, people are not manifesting the fruit of the Spirit. The Bible says in Galatians 5:22–25:

> *But the fruit of the Spirit is love, joy, peace, longsuffering, kindness, goodness, faithfulness, gentleness, self-control. Against such there is no law. And those who are Christ's have crucified the flesh with its passions and desires. If we live in the Spirit, let us also walk in the Spirit.* (NKJV)

But instead of manifesting the fruit of the Spirit, many saints today manifest its opposite. They reflect poor attitudes and self-centeredness. They sow conflict and contention. They walk in the works of the flesh.

Paul writes in Galatians 5:19–21:

> *Now the works of the flesh are evident, which are: adultery, fornication, uncleanness, lewdness, idolatry, sorcery, hatred, contentions, jealousies, outbursts of wrath, selfish ambitions, dissensions, heresies, envy, murders, drunkenness, revelries, and the like; of which I tell you beforehand, just as I also told you in time past, that those who practice such things will not inherit the kingdom of God.* (NKJV)

Paul urges us in Ephesians 4:14 to be "no longer children, tossed to and fro." Yet many believers today fail to move beyond spiritual infancy. Our churches are full of people suffering from arrested growth.

And here's the sobering truth: some people's growth is arrested because they've chosen not to grow. They don't want to mature in the things of God—because growth costs. Maturity requires you to resolve conflict, forgive, sacrifice, be the bigger person, show loyalty, and become a more responsible, reliable, committed believer and church member.

But many don't want to pay that price. It's simpler. More comfortable. More convenient—to stay immature and cling to the attitudes of a babe in Christ. However, this is not the will of God. The will of God is that we "be no longer babes, but go on to maturity."

Suffering & Sacrifice: A Part of the Mature-in-Christ Package

People in churches today want the benefits of a relationship with God without the costs. They want the pleasure without the pain. They want the glory without the struggle. They want to experience the power without the suffering. But Paul writes in Philippians 3:10–11:

> *That I may know Him and the power of His resurrection, and the fellowship of His sufferings, being conformed to His death, if by any means I may attain to the resurrection from the dead.* (NKJV)

Today's church members might say, "That's good for you, Paul. I'm not interested in joining Christ in the fellowship of His sufferings—but I'll be glad to share with Him in the power of His resurrection!" What they fail to realize is that this is a package deal.

God is not going to allow you to only partake in the power of His resurrection and ultimately rise from the dead with all the faithful saints. He's not pleased with those who are only in it for the good—who are unwilling to endure anything for Him. If you won't suffer with Him and sacrifice for Him, you're not going to reign with Him. This cannot be a one-sided relationship. You're going to have to give up something—a lot—to have a true relationship with Christ.

That means laying down your immature ways as a baby Christian, embracing discipleship, and growing up in the things of God so you can be a valuable contributor to your ministry and to the kingdom of God.

Think I'm being radical when I say you need to suffer with and for Christ? Not at all. Suffering is biblical. The writer of Hebrews says in Hebrews 5:8–9:

> *Though He was a Son, yet He learned obedience by the things which He suffered. And having been perfected, He became the author of eternal salvation to all who obey Him…* (NKJV)

Christ learned obedience through suffering, and as a result, He inherited all that the Father had for Him. He did not live His life trying to avoid suffering. In fact, suffering for us was the entire reason Christ went to Calvary!

It's clear that suffering is a biblical principle—but still, today, we convince ourselves that it's unnecessary. Some even believe suffering is anti-biblical or not the will of God at all. Yet a simple reading of Scripture reveals that going through some things is part of God's plan for our lives.

Moving on to Maturity is a Choice You Must Make!

For some reason, many of the saints don't want to go on to perfection—even though the Bible specifically tells us that this is God's expectation for our lives. For example, Hebrews 5:12 states:

> *For though by this time you ought to be teachers, you need someone to teach you again the first principles of the oracles of God; and you have come to need milk and not solid food.* (NKJV)

The term "ought to be" suggests that God has an expectation for us to advance from one level to another. He expects us to grow up in the things of God—from babes to mature believers. If that's the expectation, why aren't people in the church meeting it? Do we really think we can defy God's expectation and still be in His will?

Hebrews continues in 6:1: "Therefore, leaving the discussion of the elementary principles of Christ, let us go on to perfection…" (NKJV). Now, the word "perfection" here doesn't mean sinless, flawless, or without failure. In the Greek, it translates to "mature," "of full age," "the state of the more intelligent," or "completeness." This is what we should all be striving for as believers: growth and maturity in the things of God. Why then are we so comfortable remaining at the same level of spiritual maturity we had the day we gave our lives to Christ—even if that was years ago?

Another clear indicator that we're not maturing in the things of God is the presence of factions in the church. And this isn't anything new under the sun. The apostle Paul had to address divisions in the early church. He writes in 1 Corinthians 1:10–13:

> *Now I plead with you, brethren, by the name of our Lord Jesus Christ, that you all speak the same thing, and that there be no divisions among you, but that you be perfectly joined together in the same mind and in the same*

> *judgment. For it has been declared to me concerning you, my brethren, by those of Chloe's household, that there are contentions among you. Now I say this, that each of you says, 'I am of Paul,' or 'I am of Apollos,' or 'I am of Cephas,' or 'I am of Christ.' Is Christ divided? Was Paul crucified for you? Or were you baptized in the name of Paul?* (NKJV)

Through this passage, God makes it clear: there should be no divisions, sects, or cliques in the church. Christ is not divided—and His body should not be divided either. In light of this, we should never see people organizing themselves into closed-off groups based on their own interests, conflicts, or beliefs. The body of Christ is supposed to operate as one unit, on one accord. We're called to have one mind and the same judgment—and be "perfectly joined together." That sounds like the complete opposite of what happens when a church is full of cliques.

You might think church cliques are harmless. But trust me—I've seen what they can become. After people splinter into their groups, start having separate conversations, exclusive gatherings, and develop groupthink mentalities that may or may not align with church leadership—drama unfolds. I've witnessed it with my own eyes. People become like the Hatfields and the McCoys—which, for those unfamiliar, refers to two families who had such a famous post–Civil War feud that the entire nation took notice.

That's how church cliques can spiral. One group will approach me to weaponize my authority against another group. The bickering gets so intense that people try to pressure me into taking sides or issuing rulings that favor their clique. In some cases, they outright demand that I destroy another member—simply because that person doesn't think, believe, or operate like them. Even worse? They wouldn't lose one minute of sleep if that person were destroyed. This should not be!

The Charge to Mature and Grow Up!

It is high time for believers to grow up. Rather than live the entirety of your spiritual journey as a babe, it's time to advance beyond the babe stage and go on to maturity. Think about how concerned you would be if someone remained in the babe stage in their natural, human development. You'd likely believe something was seriously wrong with a child who was six years old but looked—and acted—like they were only one. Wouldn't you?

There is no way we can fulfill the mission of the church if it's full of people who still look and act like babes—rather than those who walk in the disposition of mature believers. So, here's the charge: *Grow up in God.* Lay aside the excuses, the immaturity, and the delays. Yes, the road to maturity requires sacrifice, discipline, and humility—but the reward is a deeper walk with Christ, a disposition that reflects His nature, and a life that honors your calling.

There's too much work to be done in the kingdom to have churches full of believers who refuse to grow. God is looking for mature saints—those who are willing to leave behind spiritual infancy and press toward the mark of the high calling in Christ Jesus. If we truly want to be effective, powerful, Spirit-led believers, we must make the daily choice to grow up and live like it.

The church doesn't just need attendees. *It needs mature disciples.* And the decision to move on to maturity is one only *you* can make. Let's get to it.

6

The Malpractice of Ministry Leaders Lacking Maturity

Unfortunately, I have noticed that many times, we pride ourselves in leadership on how many people get put out of the church. In our eyes, over the years, that is what made us holy: we see people in sin, and we get it out of God's church. However, based on this standard, every person in the church has something—if made known to others—that would qualify them to be put out of the church too, including the leader. So what are we doing? I submit to you that putting people out of the church simply because their struggle was exposed is not a sign of holiness; it is a failure. It demonstrates a lack of maturity.

Now, this is not to say that we should never put anyone out of the church. Is excommunication necessary at times? Undoubtedly. However, these occasions should be rare and only occur in the most extreme situations—when a person habitually engages in wrongdoing, and after leadership has made every effort to work with and support them, they still appear to be beyond repentance.

If that is not the case—and we are simply dealing with a struggling saint who sincerely desires to be different—let's do as Paul says in Romans 15:1a: "We then that are strong ought to bear the infirmities of the weak" (KJV). Notice that Paul didn't say to throw them away.

Why are we so quick to dismiss our brothers and sisters in Christ, especially when they are struggling and need our spiritual support, prayers, and encouragement more than ever? This is a heartbreaker for me in ministry. I genuinely desire to see the people of God love each other well.

t's not just lay people who have some maturing to do. Sometimes we pastors are guilty of malpractice, and the leaders under us are just as guilty—because we fail to fully embrace our role to restore, repair, and recover. It's because we forget those moments when we were broken and needed to be supported and restored ourselves. This isn't just an issue in holiness churches; I've seen this leadership shortcoming across all types of churches. The longer I've been around, the more I've found that leaders tend to operate with selective righteousness and selective judgment regarding who they choose to castigate.

When I think about how people without the disposition of a mature believer mishandle situations in the church, I think back to a time when I was a youngster who hadn't been saved long. I'll never forget it. I was probably a teenager at the time, sitting in church. Some of my peers had gotten into trouble—not anything major, just the typical antics of mischievous young men. A few of the boys had gone to the pastor for help—for support and guidance on how to work through the situation.

Well, when they went to church that Sunday morning, the pastor basically preached about them and the trouble they'd gotten into. He didn't mention names, but the people close to the situation knew exactly who he was talking about. Then he said, "I told these individuals that I do believe the Lord forgave them, but I have to put them out of the church." Even as a young believer listening from the pew, I was sitting there bewildered. Something in my spirit said, "This doesn't make any sense. If the Lord forgave them, why would you put them out?"

The truth is, that pastor was focused on externals. It was about him, not about them. As the leader, he wanted to present himself as someone who didn't tolerate any unholiness in the church—even if it came from mischievous teenagers. Sadly, some of those young men never recovered after being put out. Only one made it back to the things of God. The damage had been done. It was so sad. It was heartbreaking.

Another example that comes to mind involved me. Years ago, when I had only been pastoring a few weeks, a brother who had been restored joined our church. But he struggled with an addiction to alcohol. I was so determined to make my mark as a brand-new pastor in a conservative city, I fellowshipped him into the church one week—and disfellowshipped him the very next week. I thought I had done something commendable—putting someone with a moral struggle out of the church.

As time went on and I matured in ministry, I looked back at that moment with great anguish and shame. I should've helped that young man. We as a church should have helped him—not thrown him away. I should not have allowed the congregation to pressure me into acting prematurely. But in my immaturity, I was more concerned about my image in their eyes than about being the shepherd God called me to be. It's one of my greatest regrets—but I've learned to give myself grace. I was young, and I was silly.

Years ago, a senior bishop shared a story with me that's stuck with me ever since. When he was a young district elder, there was a young minister in his church going through some challenges. To address the matter, he brought the young man in—along with several other leaders: ministers, bishops, and elders. They all gathered in the room and observed while he laid out the details of the situation with the young minister.

The case against the minister didn't look very good. Once the facts and details about the case had been fully laid out, the district elder who had called everyone together for the gathering dismissed himself; he had to step out to go teach a class. Before he left the room, he advised the other leaders there to stay and keep talking to the young minister. Well, by the time the district elder finished his class and came back to the room, the leaders had disfellowshipped the young man, putting him out of the church.

He looked at them and asked, "You put him out of my church? Why would you guys do that? You blew it!" They didn't understand. He said, "If I had wanted to put him out of the church, I would have just put him out! I brought the case before you all so you could help save him, not throw him away!" When these leaders had the opportunity to show compassion, they did not. The leader's intent was to preserve his young minister. However, he'd invited the other leaders to the proceedings because he didn't want to put his hands on the situation; if he had restored the young man himself, people might have thought he was too soft in addressing unholiness or in the church. The whole thing just backfired badly.

7

Going on to Perfection: Making the Commitment to Grow Into a Mature Believer

In order for us to be all that God intended for us to become when He saved us, a shift is necessary. We've already examined Romans 12:1–2, in which the apostle Paul makes a plea to us to make such a shift, saying:

> *I beseech you therefore, brethren, by the mercies of God, that you present your bodies a living sacrifice, holy,*

acceptable to God, which is your reasonable service. And do not be conformed to this world, but be transformed by the renewing of your mind, that you may prove what is that good and acceptable and perfect will of God." (NKJV)

To manifest the disposition of the believer, we need to experience an internal shift; our minds and our thought patterns need to change. God wants us dying while we are living. Everything in us that's not like God must die. All of our external change begins with the transformation of the mind. The disposition of the believer—the mature believer—comes when we allow the Holy Spirit to replace our own temperamentally driven, selfishly motivated thinking with the principles of the Word of God. It comes when we allow the mind of Christ to be in us (Philippians 2:5). We must accept that we have no right to think what we want; we must think the thoughts of Christ in order to manifest the character of Christ in our lives.

If we want our churches to have the impact of the first-century saints to whom Paul was writing in Romans 12:1–2—those who endured persecution and persevered in spreading the gospel of the kingdom of God against all odds—we need to think differently and be different. We must dedicate ourselves decisively as a living sacrifice. Life can no longer be about us. We must shake off this 21st-century spirit of self-centered entitlement, immaturity, and carnality and do as Hebrews 6:1 instructs us to do: leave the elementary principles of Christ and go on to perfection, or maturity. Let's all commit to moving on to manifest the disposition of the believer, because until we embrace a disposition motivated by love, selflessness, and sacrifice, we will never be suitable to be used by God.

How to Move on to Perfection

You might be asking, "Bishop, how do I become more mature? How do I begin growing to manifest the true disposition of a believer?"

Prayer

The first thing I recommend is that you start praying the prayer of the psalmist: "Lord, make me to know my end, and what is the measure of my days, that I may know how frail I am" (Psalm 39:4, NKJV). This should be the daily prayer of all believers. If you truly desire to see yourself, God will show you. I believe God's revelation of who we are to ourselves is gradual. If He showed us all of ourselves—including all of our flaws and all areas where we need transformation—at one time, we would get so frustrated that we would give up. This is why God only allows layers to be peeled back little by little so that the revelation is not too overwhelming.

Seeing all the parts of who we truly are is a lifelong project. Even at the end of the journey, He still needs to bring grace with Him when He returns for us. This does not give us permission to stay as we are. Instead, we must say, "I press toward the goal for the prize of the upward call of God in Christ Jesus" (Philippians 3:14, NKJV). To become a mature believer who manifests the disposition of a believer, you must press. This means you must understand and continually battle against resistance as you strive to become all that Christ expects you to be.

Self-reflection

We must engage in self-reflection so that we see ourselves for who we really are. If you never know who you really are, you will never know what you need to become in order to manifest the disposition of the believer that God intended for you. When you truly see yourself as a believer, if you see yourself as spotless and near-perfect, you are deceived. We are far from where God desires for us to be in relation to the character of Christ.

Thus, self-reflection is a big part of achieving the disposition of the believer. It is a key ingredient in striving to become Christ-like. The only one who can show you is God, but you must be open to the process and willing to accept rather than dismiss what you see. This requires relinquishing your pride and self-righteousness. Accept that you are flawed and that you fall short, and ask God to help you become spiritually transformed. Accept that "But we are all like an unclean thing, and all our righteousnesses are like filthy rags" (Isaiah 64:6a, KJV). Self-reflection is all a part of the cycle of growing to know and knowing to grow. It swings back and forth. Our eyes are jaded toward ourselves, so we must invite the power of God to show us to ourselves.

Refusing to Conform to the World

In Romans 12:2, Paul instructs us to "not be conformed to this world, but be transformed by the renewing of your mind..." (NKJV). If we're going to have the right disposition as saints, we need to ask ourselves: Who should have the most influence over our lives? The answer is simple: God should. He should influence every aspect of our lives. Ask yourself,

Is God truly the most influential force in my life? If He's not, then something or someone else is influencing you. You'll never be able to manifest the disposition of the believer if you are not intentional about conforming to Christ.

If you don't conform to God, you will conform to the world. Worldly influence might seem harmless, but Satan is never harmless. He can present himself as an angel of light, but he remains a deceiver. He even goes to church every Sunday, catching those of us who aren't alert and aware. God didn't save us so we could be molded by the world. He saved us to restore us to His image and manifest the character of Christ.

Bearing His image sets us apart, and being set apart can make you a target. It means you can't fit in everywhere or with everyone. Sometimes, God doesn't want you to be friends with certain people because those relationships can rob you of His image, His glory, and His favor. If there's anything—an association, a habit, a desire—pulling you away from God, let it go. Ask the Lord to restore His image in you and help you to be conformed to Christ so you can lead a life that reflects the God inside you.

Acknowledgement of Our Sinfulness

Most believers really don't understand the depth of sin and the sin condition. Paul writes in Romans 7:24, "O wretched man that I am! Who will deliver me from this body of death?" (NKJV) In order to progress toward manifesting the disposition of the believer, we must be willing to acknowledge that as saved as we may be, we are housed in a wretched, sinful vessel—the body. The body in which we live propels our thoughts, appetites, impulses, and desires—the very ones that drive us to sin and cause us to turn around and find ourselves in trouble. We are so fallen that we can't even see how far down we have fallen. We can't see how deep the grip of sin is in us. When He shows it to us, we must repent, die to ourselves, and allow the character of Christ to shine through.

Extending the Grace You've Received to Others

I know that even as we grow more and more mature in Christ, we are never going to be grown until Christ returns and gets us out of here. I also know that even though we might become more mature year by year, none of us will ever reach the point of flawlessness or literal perfection. One of my personal sayings, which I call "Gatesisms," is this: If Jesus doesn't bring some grace with Him when He returns, none of us is getting out of here! We've all got to pray that He brings grace with Him, because we all need it, from the pulpit to the pews. In light of this, how much more grace should we extend to our brothers and sisters? Christ has already given us so much grace—not only to save us, but every day since the moment we were saved. If we truly appreciate what He has done for us, we should do the same for others.

A Call to Commit to the Transformation

As we bring this journey to a close, I want to leave you with one final charge: commit to the transformation that God has set before you. The truths we have explored together are not meant to remain within the pages of this book; they are meant to become living realities in your everyday life. The disposition of the mature believer is not an abstract ideal; it is the evidence of a life surrendered to Christ—a life that reflects His love, grace, and selflessness. Now is the time to take everything you have read, meditate on it, and actively pursue the change that the Holy Spirit is working within you.

Remember, this journey of maturity is not about achieving perfection in your own strength. It is about allowing the Holy Spirit to continually refine you, renew your mind, and transform your heart so that Christ's character shines through you. It is about yielding to His process and embracing the truth that His grace is sufficient, even in your weakness. There will be moments when the call to maturity feels overwhelming, when your disposition does not align with the image of Christ as it should. In those moments, do not lose heart. Press forward, knowing that God's power is made perfect in your weakness and that His Spirit will complete the work He has begun in you.

As you strive to manifest the disposition of the believer, understand that this is not just a personal pursuit; it is a kingdom mandate. Your transformation is not only for your benefit, but also for the sake of those who are watching your life, seeking a glimpse of the Christ you profess to follow. When you allow the mind of Christ to influence your thoughts and actions, you become a living testimony of God's love and power. Your kindness, patience, and selflessness have the potential to draw others into the light of His truth. By embodying the character of Christ, you participate in lifting Him up so that He may draw all people to Himself.

Finally, let us remember that the goal of spiritual maturity is not merely to "do better," but to truly reflect Christ in all that we are. This reflection requires daily self-reflection, humility, and a commitment to conforming to God's Word rather than the world around us. It is a lifelong journey that demands perseverance and grace, but the reward is eternal. My prayer is that this book has not only challenged you, but also equipped you to grow deeper in your faith and closer to the image of Christ. May your life be a beacon of His love, and may your disposition be a testimony that glorifies God and draws others to His kingdom.

Let us go forward together, pressing toward the mark for the prize of the high calling in Christ Jesus—for His glory and the good of His church.

www.ingramcontent.com/pod-product-compliance
Lightning Source LLC
Chambersburg PA
CBHW050654160426
43194CB00010B/1939